INFLUENCE PEOPLE

MAKE THE OTHER PERSON FEEL IMPORTANT

ARVIND UPADHYAY

Let me share one quick story. I know a single lady in her 60s who is an important person. She's divorced, has two grown kids and a couple of grandkids. She has a regular job and struggles to make ends meet like most people these days. She likes working in her yard and around her home and she's always willing to help others. She's a nice person, a nice neighbor to those who live near her. She's not done anything that will make her famous but she's important nonetheless. Who is this person? My mom, Ann Strausburg. If it were not for her I would not be here and you wouldn't be reading this. My wife Jane might be married to someone else and my wonderful daughter Abigail would not have come into existence. From my limited perspective my mom is very important and I'm sure from God's view, because He knows her full impact, He'd say she's incredibly important!

I hope everyone treats my mom with the kind of respect she deserves. I bet you hope the same for your mom, dad, grandparents, kids or anyone else who is significant to you. If we hope that then we should do that. Every day as we meet people if we make them feel import they'll sense that. Of course they'll like us for it too.

Don't you enjoy it when people treat you like you're important? It can be humbling at times but I know I enjoy it and I bet you do too. If we enjoy it then why not spread the joy and allow others to feel the same way? Here are a few simple things anyone can do to convey a sense of importance to another person:

Show respect – Respect comes easily through good manners with phrases like, "Yes please," "No thank you," "Excuse me" and "Please forgive me." These are simple and none assumes anything from the other person.

Use their name – As I shared in the article A Rose by Any Other Name, the sweetest sound to any person is the sound of their own name. People feel important when identified by name because it humanizes them.

Golden Rule – Treat people the way you'd like to be treated or the way you'd like someone to treat a loved one. This kind of behavior tends to come back to you. Earl Hickey calls it karma.

Fine Reputation – We will explore Carnegie's advice to give the other person a fine reputation to live up to later in this series. For now know this; conveying belief in another person can help them achieve more than they thought possible and make them feel more important than ever before. Give that gift.

We make requests of people every single day because we need other people. Recognizing that fact, this blog is intended to help you learn to hear "Yes!" The more friends you make, the easier it is to influence people and hear "Yes!" But it's not just about getting what you want. It's about building relationships and enjoying our lives more because of those relationships. Make another person feel important today and that's one step in the right direction them and for you.

Contents

Foreword   *vii*

1. Techniques In Handling People   1

2. How To Become Friends With Someone (fast)   13

3. Criticism Is Futile   19

4. Give People What They Want   22

5. Summary Of How To Win Friends And Influence People   29

14 Ways to Make People Feel Important

Listen to them. When they are talking to you, really listen. Make eye contact, close your mouth, and focus on the words they are saying, not on what you want to say the moment they stop talking. Take the time to really listen to them.

Show your admiration. When we tell someone we admire something about them, it signals that we value who they are and the choices they have made, which tends to make people feel good.

Be appreciative. Something else Mary Kay said was, "Everyone wants to be appreciated, so if you appreciate someone, don't keep it a secret."

Notice things. Make a note of something that they did well recently and point it out to them; explain why you think it's great. Compliment them on something they are wearing or doing; it's surprising the things we can see when we open our eyes.

Use their name. As Dale Carnegie will tell you, people really love to hear the sound of their own name, so say it out loud, personalize your conversation with it, and connect it with something good that they have done.

Connect on a deeper level. Invest the time to get beyond the superficial and learn about the person – ask about their families, favorite hobbies, and what gets them excited outside the work environment.

Follow up. Whether it's a question they had, a big event in their lives, or something they needed help with, follow up with them. When we make the effort to get back to them with answers, or simply to find out how their big fishing weekend went, it tells them they are important to us.

See the potential. If you see promise in their abilities, mention it to them, then help them find a path to develop their potential; suggest books to read, courses to take, and experiences that could help them grow.

Ask them to teach you. Find something they are good at and ask them to show you how they do it. This honors their accomplishments, while making you smarter at the same time. In fact, this is a good way for a new leader to quickly build credibility and expertise.

Give them the credit. When they are right about something, acknowledge it publicly.

Trust them with the truth. Respect them enough to be honest with them; tell them that's what you are doing.

Value their time. Show up on time for meetings, come prepared, and stay focused.

Align them with the mission. There should be a clear linkage between what each person on your team does, and how the mission gets accomplished. Talk with them about how their actions are critical to advancing the team. If you find this difficult, it might be time to review roles and responsibilities.

And vitally, there's this:

Be honest. Only say it if it's true and if you mean it. People can sense insincerity from a mile away, so don't insult them with platitudes and meaningless words.

14 Ways to Make People Feel Important

Listen to them. When they are talking to you, really listen. Make eye contact, close your mouth, and focus on the words they are saying, not on what you want to say the moment they stop talking. Take the time to really listen to them.

Show your admiration. When we tell someone we admire something about them, it signals that we value who they are and the choices they have made, which tends to make people feel good.

Be appreciative. Something else Mary Kay said was, "Everyone wants to be appreciated, so if you appreciate someone, don't keep it a secret."

Notice things. Make a note of something that they did well recently and point it out to them; explain why you think it's great. Compliment them on something they are wearing or doing; it's surprising the things we can see when we open our eyes.

Use their name. As Dale Carnegie will tell you, people really love to hear the sound of their own name, so say it out loud, personalize your conversation with it, and connect it with something good that they have done.

Connect on a deeper level. Invest the time to get beyond the superficial and learn about the person – ask about their families, favorite hobbies, and what gets them excited outside the work environment.

Follow up. Whether it's a question they had, a big event in their lives, or something they needed help with, follow up with them. When we make the effort to get back to them with answers, or simply to find out how their big fishing weekend went, it tells them they are important to us.

See the potential. If you see promise in their abilities, mention it to them, then help them find a path to develop their potential; suggest books to read, courses to take, and experiences that could help them grow.

Ask them to teach you. Find something they are good at and ask them to show you how they do it. This honors their accomplishments, while making you smarter at the same time. In fact, this is a good way for a new leader to quickly build credibility and expertise.

Give them the credit. When they are right about something, acknowledge it publicly.

Trust them with the truth. Respect them enough to be honest with them; tell them that's what you are doing.

Value their time. Show up on time for meetings, come prepared, and stay focused.

Align them with the mission. There should be a clear linkage between what each person on your team does, and how the mission gets accomplished. Talk with them about how their actions are critical to advancing the team. If you find this difficult, it might be time to review roles and responsibilities.

And vitally, there's this:

Be honest. Only say it if it's true and if you mean it. People can sense insincerity from a mile away, so don't insult them with platitudes and meaningless words.

1

Techniques in Handling People

To handle people well, we must never criticize, condemn or complain because it will never result in the behavior we desire. Give honest and sincere appreciation. Appreciation is one of the most powerful tools in the world.Your "people skills" & ability to effectively communicate to/with others is arguably one of the most important factors in your level of success. Whether you're the CEO of a prospering organization, a professional salesperson, or a full-time mom — your ability to influence people is key to your success in any endeavor.

1.) Don't criticize, condemn, or complain.

Now this 1st rule should be an obvious one! Nobody likes people who constantly criticize, condemn, or complain.

We as humans do not like to admit fault — it's human nature. When people are criticized or humiliated, they rarely respond well and will often become defensive and resent their critic.

To successfully influence others, we must be very cautious of how what we say might effect our counterparts. Whether it's speaking directly to someone or just making a comment not directed at anybody, it'd be beneficial to remain mindful of what you say.

For example, if you're a real pessimistic person, people will resent being in your presence because they know that you're going to eventually lower their level of happiness & joy by seeing the worst in everything.

Or if you're the leader who is constantly criticizing your staff or your team, you'll end up having a hard time influencing them to produce the behavior you desire because they will never feel comfortable around you.

When you criticize, condemn, and complain, you are clearly putting relationship points in the debit column. You more than likely know people who do this all too frequently. They are the kind of folks who light up the room only when they leave. Gary Player, the professional golfer, once said, "Some people think their own candle burns brighter when they snuff out other people's candles."

Not only does criticism have a negative effect on personal relationships, it can also destroy business relationships. In one of our training programs we ask people to share an experience that they could "buy back" if they could. The following story is one of the more powerful.

An individual worked for a local construction company. He was driving on the Beltline on a nice summer day in a company pickup with the company logo on both sides of the truck. All of a sudden he was passed and almost sideswiped by a little, red, two-seater Mercedes, driven by an attractive lady. Not to be outdone, and apparently to justify his manhood, he caught up to her and did exactly the same thing to her. To put an exclamation point on the maneuver, he actually flipped her off as he passed and made darn sure she saw the gesture.

Later that day when he got back to the shop, his boss called him to his office. The boss basically repeated the part of the story about him going after the Mercedes. He also said that the woman had been about to sign a significant remodeling contract with the company. Not only was she now NOT going to sign the contract, she promised that she would tell all her friends the story, along with the strong recommendation to never do business with the company.

Does criticism have an impact on business relationships? Duh!

It was Dale Carnegie who said, "Any fool can criticize, condemn, or complain." What he did not say is how many of us fall into the foolish trap and put those negative points in the debit column of personal and professional relationships. In today's fast-paced electronic world, I cannot tell you how many stories I have heard about those who have hit "Reply All" in a highly emotional state and regretted it the moment they took their finger off the SEND button. An old friend of mine used to have a saying that reiterates the point:

"Be careful of the words you speak,
Keep them soft and sweet,
Because you'll never know from day to day,
Which ones you'll have to eat."

I know some of you are saying, "What about constructive criticism?" Yes, there are times when it is important to let another person know that their behavior or way of doing a task needs improvement. In fact, my previous blog addressed exactly that issue. See "Constructive Criticism: A Few Tips on the Constructive Part."

if the goal is build and maintain — not destroy — long-term personal and business relationships, it is probably a good idea to stay away from criticism, condemnation, and complaining.

When Dale Carnegie began teaching 100 years ago, nobody, not even he could imagine what has become of his legacy. Carnegie taught hundreds of lectures to thousands of students who sought the wisdom he had learned to harness.

He developed a set of thirty principles in a codex called "<u>How to Win Friends and Influence People</u>" 75 years ago that iterated his philosophy on how to win friends and influence people. Ask anyone, even current CEO of the Carnegie Empire, Peter Handal and he'll <u>tell</u> you that the elder Carnegie's secret to success was influencing people. "You can change people's behavior by changing your attitude towards them," said Handal of Carnegie's philosophy.

100 years later, <u>Dale Carnegie Training</u> works to provide leaders and employees in corporations and government agencies with the skills necessary to influence people the exact same way Dale Carnegie himself prescribed those skills. Dale Carnegie Training allows teams and individuals the opportunity to attend leadership training seminars as well.

The first principle that Dale Carnegie offered to his audience was "**Don't criticize, condemn, or complain**." This ideal teaches us to be kind and thoughtful when considering other peoples' feelings. Its about showing respect to get respect – treating others the way you want to be treated. This principle encourages an open mind when talking other people.

Don't criticize a person for having a different opinion than you because everyone's opinion matters regardless of whether there is 100 percent agreement. If you skip right to criticizing, you will never get anything accomplished. The most common natural reaction for someone is to clam up and shy away from a conversation with you. This is especially important in the workplace when trying to settle a conflict. Conflict resolution does not happen by criticizing your fellow team members.

Don't condemn your coworker or friend for doing something you don't believe was right. There may be a reason why he or she decided to do things that way. And you won't know that unless you approach your friend with an open mind and a cool head. Condemning another person's actions without knowing the full circumstance of that action is immature and short-sighted.

Don't complain about a decision that was made or about a problem you are having. Instead work actively to solve it. Ask yourself what's the worst that could possibly happen, and then look for a solution. Someone once told me that 'complacency is the enemy of progress.' Complaining about your job or something that happened is going to prevent you from solving the problem and its going to get you a lot of annoyed looks from your cohorts. People don't want to hear you complain about something that happened in the past, they want to hear *how* or *what* you did to solve it.

Without jumping to conclusions, I task you to apply this principle to your life. Look closely at the difference between the two options afterwards and post a comment here letting us know how it turned out. If you follow this guideline, you will feel less stressed and more willing to try this again in the future because it worked for you once before. I encourage you to try this because you'll walk away from the situation with a good feeling, a high level of productivity and a positive working relationship with your coworker.

Criticism is utile because it puts a person on the defensive and usually makes him strive to justify himself. Criticism is dangerous, because it wounds a person's precious pride, hurts his sense of importance, and arouses resentment.

by criticizing, we do not make lasting changes, and often incur resentment.

Any fool can criticize, condemn and complain — and most fools do. But it takes character and self-control to be understanding and forgiving.

Instead of condemning people, try to understand them. Try to figure out why they do what they do. that's a lot more profitable and intriguing than criticism; and in breeds sympathy, tolerance and kindness. "To know all is to forgive all."

It's so easy to criticize other people, and so hard to give a single honest compliment. It's so easy to see yourself in a good light and at the same time focus on imperfections of other people.

But criticizing people is a complete lose-lose situation that only creates distance, spreads negative energies and causes tensions. Criticism is one of the worst kinds of negative thinking, talking and acting.

If positive thoughts are creative thoughts of connecting, including, sharing and loving, then negative thinking is composed of thoughts and words (and consequently actions) that disconnect, exclude and spread hate.

Since it's impossible to live a positive life with a negative mind, it's obvious why criticizing others is so unproductive and irrational. So let's put a stop to it.

WHY DO YOU LOVE TO CRITICIZE PEOPLE?

On a logical level, we probably all know that criticizing people brings no good to anybody. And yet we still do it. If you do it, that means it must bring you some kind of value or benefit. Well, it does in the short term. The benefits are of emotional nature, and emotions are most often stronger than logic.

That means you must understand criticizing other people on an emotional level, to deal with it once and for all. So let's analyze the most frequent reasons why we all love to criticize other people so much and have a hard time resisting it.

There is no rational benefits in criticizing other people. But emotional short-term benefits (that quickly backfire) are always present.

YOU CRITICIZE PEOPLE TO CREATE EMOTIONAL DISTANCE

We are often more kind to strangers than we are to our loved ones. Many couples, parents or siblings are very critical towards each other. Most often the emotional reason for that is to create distance in a relationship. Criticism is a great way to emotionally distance yourself from another person.

Now, why would you want to do that? Well, because on the subconscious level you are afraid to be hurt or disappointed. Kids leave their nests, siblings can be more successful than you, your spouse might break your heart, and so on.

By criticizing others and focusing on their imperfections, you can emotionally protect yourself at least a little bit (they're sour grapes – more about that later).

Understanding that leads us to only one important conclusion. It's ridiculous to create distance by criticizing others. By criticizing you are ironically forcing them to hurt you sooner or later.

Nobody likes to be criticized; and obviously nobody can hurt you more than your negative untamed mind can. Thus, there is no need to create distance, only to improve your thoughts, feeling of self-worth and turn critiques into praise.

On the other hand, sometimes we even use criticism to create connections and closeness with other people. That is in cases when we look for a common enemy to consequently find common ground with somebody we like or can benefit from.

But starting a relationship based on hate is absolutely not a good start. We're only showing off what we are prepared to do to other people, just to get a little bit of attention and love. Negative energies always somehow escalate and backfire.

You probably love to criticize other people because you were criticized a lot as a young person.

The second most frequent reason why people criticize others is to feel better about themselves. If someone's success or personality is too shiny, it's easy to throw dirt at it, and the shininess instantly loses its brightness. At least a little bit; in our eyes. What a relief. Not.

It's been statistically proven that we are very indulgent towards ourselves and much harsher and judging towards others. We have double standards to protect our egos.If somebody is better in something important to us or owns something we want or outruns us in a competition, we must quickly find all the reasons why they aren't as good as they appear; otherwise we feel humiliated.

YOU CRITICIZE OTHER PEOPLE BECAUSE YOU ENVY THEM

Criticizing others to feel better about yourself and criticizing out of envy are closely connected motives. They are a slightly different tones of the same voice. Let me explain.

It's in our genes to hate unfairness. And when somebody gets something we want in a very unfair way, or when we feel life was unfair to us and kind to others, brutally strong feelings of envy arise.

Examples of situations that usually make us envious, because life is unfair:

A friend gets lucky and earns much more money, much more easily than we do

A parent shows more attention to a sibling than to us

A coworker gets promoted, but we obviously deserve the promotion more

A colleague is talented and doesn't have to work so hard to be good at a certain sport

We offer much better support to our kids than we had, but it seems they don't appreciate it

We can find many similar situations

All these situations are very unfair. Well, life can be extremely unfair sometimes and that hurts. We protect ourselves with many different rationalization mechanisms. We protect ourselves with self-delusion.

"Sour grapes" and "sweet lemons" are two very frequent rationalization mechanisms. With self-deception, you make things that you want but don't have less desirable (sour grapes) and things that you do have but are not that important to you more desirable (sweet lemons).

Criticizing others is absolutely a way to make grapes less sweet – to make other people's accomplishments less worthy, to make relationships less important, and what other people have irrelevant.

In a way, we could say that criticizing others is often an easy way to express frustrations and other negative emotions. But criticizing other people or complaining won't help. Only a superior life strategy and going into action to improve your life will.

YOU DON'T ACCEPT THAT PEOPLE HAVE DIFFERENT LEVELS OF CAPABILITIES

Very capable and highly organized people usually have zero tolerance towards less capable people. They very strictly judge and criticize others when they do something wrong or don't meet their standards. I used to be one of them (and still am a little bit).

The reason behind that is that usually these people were severely judged in their upbringing. Consequently, they set extremely high demands for themselves and others. It's an internalized judging voice of parents that haunts you (inner critic) and is also directed towards others (outer critic).

In such a mental model, we don't realize that people have different capabilities. We don't take into account that people have different levels of experience, competence and that maybe not all were raised to high perfectionist standards.

That doesn't mean you must lower your standards, but criticizing others is rarely the way that leads to improved performance of other people. It sooner leads to hate than improvement.

Criticism is an indirect form of self-boasting. – Emmet Fox

A COMPLETE LOSE-LOSE SITUATION

Nobody gains anything from criticizing. The other person feels devaluated. It creates distance and decreases capacity for love. With criticism, you easily spread the negative energy around and destroy other people's days.

People rarely listen to criticism, even if it's justified, and they don't try to improve themselves. Instead they take it personally and then avoid you, cut you out of their lives or criticize you back.

With criticism, you might feel a little bit better about yourself and your ego might feel a bit safer, but at what price? You are doing damage to relationships, your mental health (negative thoughts) and you are trampling the other person's potential and provoke their inner peace.

You are pushing people away from your life. You are depriving yourself and others of love. That is a huge price to pay for feeling a little better about yourself in the short term.

Sometimes you criticize people to help them, sometimes to hurt them. In both cases, you are doing damage to yourself and other people. There are better ways to help others or your ego and feeling of self-worth.

TRANSFORMING CRITICISM INTO MORE CONSTRUCTIVE THOUGHTS, WORDS AND ACTIONS

Now that you know the real problems and cause of criticism, let's look at a few solutions for transforming criticism into more constructive thoughts, words and actions. There is the long-term, harder way to deal with the desire to criticize people, and a few short-term shortcuts and hacks.

The long-term way is all about developing better self-esteem and self-worth, and a greater capacity for love. When you love yourself more, you can truly start loving others; and consequently you can stop criticizing them at every step they make. If you don't feel threatened, there is no need to criticize.

With higher self-esteem, there is no need to create so much distance in relationships or trample others. Because you know your high worth and you know you will survive and be fine (maybe even thrive), it doesn't matter if somebody is better than you or that they might emotionally hurt you some day in the future.

The best short-term way to deal with criticism is to use the "switch" approach. You switch from a bad habit (criticism) to a good one (praise).

In practical terms, that means that every time you want to criticize a person, you bite your tongue (really hard) and do the following – mentor the person, find something to compliment, try to understand why the person is acting as they are, or make a conscious decision to mind your own business.

RATHER THAN CRITICIZE, SHOW PEOPLE HOW TO DO THINGS

Every time you want to criticize somebody because they didn't meet your standards, show them how to do things better – mentor them. Just say, you did an excellent job (or parts of it); I have several additional ideas, let me show you …

Or use the sandwich technique. Find something to compliment in their work, then show them what and how to do better, and end your talk by praising the person again. And if you roll your eyes while showing other people how to improve, you're doing it wrong.

Besides that, be careful when showing people how to do things. Make sure that your way really is more efficient, effective, profitable or better in a certain important standard. There are many ways how to achieve the same goal, and who says your way really is the best.

If you don't have data or metrics as a proof that your way is the right one or if you aren't sharing small tricks of industry masters, maybe you are the one who can learn something from the other person.

RATHER THAN CRITICIZE, SHOW RESPECT OR MIND YOUR OWN BUSINESS

Every time you want to criticize others with the goal of dirtying their shiny success or luck, bite your tongue and instead find a way to even deepen the relationship with that person. Find a way to develop a new dimension.

If their success is based on hard work, just think of what you can learn from them. Ask them if they are prepared to mentor you or give you some tips to be more successful.

If you envy them their (unjust) luck, well, it won't help you with your luck in life in any way. Rather than drowning in envy and criticism, brainstorm how you can get luckier in life. Do it based on the quote: the harder and smarter I work, the luckier I get. As an alternative, you can also think of all the things that you have and are grateful for.

Other people's luck doesn't mean your misfortune, if you have the abundance mindset. Life is not a zero sum game. Wealth and luck can always be created. With the abundance mindset, you know that sooner or later, you will also get lucky, as long as you stay proactive and positive enough.

Be happy when other people are struck by luck, and while you are happy, mind your own business and mind your own luck.

Any fool can criticize, condemn, and complain but it takes character and self-control to be understanding and forgiving. – Dale Carnegie

PRAISE OR SHOW EMPATHY RATHER THAN CRITICIZE

Last but not least, every time you want to criticize someone's personality, instead find something to praise. If you manage to achieve 7 compliments for every critique, you will dramatically improve your relationships with others and with yourself.

The same millisecond you think of a critique make sure you don't say it and start searching for something to praise.

If a person's extroversion bothers you, find something they're wearing that you can compliment

If a person's negativity bothers you, find something that they did well and tell them

If a person's pimple in the middle of their face bothers you, find a body part you like on them and focus on that

Physical traits, character, competences, there are so many different things you can compliment – if you just invest a little bit of effort. Remember, you are criticizing others to create distance, protect your ego, and because you are a hard judge towards yourself.

Once you stop being hard on others and focus on their positive traits, you will also focus on positive things on yourself. Consequently, you will develop greater self-confidence and capacity for love. You will become more tolerant towards yourself and towards others. What a blessing.

One more extremely powerful weapon against criticism is empathy. First, let's define what empathy is. You mustn't confuse it with sympathy or support. Sympathy means having the capacity to feel the same way as somebody else. Acting in a tender, understanding manner and standing by their side is a form of support. They are both useful, but not as powerful as empathy.

Empathy means being able to precisely understand other people's thoughts and actions, and where their actions and behaviors are coming from. When you deeply understand the context, you know the motives and what is really going on in a certain life situation. Then there is no need to criticize, only to forgive, understand or find a way to fix things.

By developing empathy, you become more tolerant and respect the diversity that life has to offer. Maybe you would be or act the same if you had the exact same life circumstances. Understand, mentor, or develop new relationship dimensions and forget about criticizing.

When you judge others, you do not define them, you define yourself. – Earl Nightingale

CONCLUDING THOUGHTS ON CRITICISM

Openly criticizing anyone, or even doing it behind their back, is very destructive behavior that spreads misery in your life and the life of people who surround you. It's impossible to live a happy and successful life with a negative mind and by spreading negative energies.

There are better ways to operate in relationships than criticizing. There are ways to transform the desire for criticism into subtler energies and more constructive actions.

You transform criticism into more positive energies, words and actions, by making sure that:

You understand there are many ways to achieve the same thing, and maybe yours is not the best.

If you know a better way, show people how to do it, don't criticize them.

If something bothers you on a person, it's usually something you don't like about yourself; or you need to understand their context and life circumstances better.

With self-delusion of how you are better than others, you won't get far in improving your life situation. Only with self-improvement, by minding your own business and working hard you can become luckier and happier.

You have to be little to belittle others. Thus criticizing others only shows you have to work on your feeling of self-worth and self-esteem.

Severely criticizing others means you are creating distance in relationships and that you have a low capacity for love. Ironically, you are forcing people into behavior that you're afraid will happen to you. Stop it.

The moment you start excluding others, creating distance and spreading negative energies, switch your thinking and acting to a more positive one. The same millisecond you want to criticize, switch to and ignite thoughts of connecting, sharing, love, praise, tolerance, compassion and empathy.

2.) *Give honest and sincere appreciation.*

Appreciation is one of the most powerful tools in the world. People will rarely work at their maximum potential under criticism, but honest appreciation brings out their best. Appreciation, though, is not simple flattery, it must be sincere, meaningful and with love.

Think about a time somebody openly acknowledged you for something that you did well. Or when someone mentions one of your strengths — something you yourself know you're great at.

Sincere appreciation isn't throwing out a bland compliment like "Great job, keep up the good work!" — it's really taking the time to notice a quality or result that an individual brings that sets himself/herself apart from the rest.

When you do receive a genuine compliment, how does it make you feel?

I personally feel very good about myself. I feel like all the work I'm doing means something and that it's affecting people's lives positively. It puts me in the right state of mind; when this happens it reminds me of why I'm doing whatever it is I'm doing and why it's important to keep improving.

It puts me in a better mood which will in turn produce better quality work & a more positive attitude. And I believe that one or more of these feelings or thoughts cross your mind as well when you receive sincere appreciation.

Aside from work — the same goes for married couples. If you're consistently reminding your spouse of something that they're doing good or ways that they're helping you out, it will in turn influence them to keep doing that good thing — and even feel good while doing it!

So, make sure you're giving out more sincere appreciation to everyone you know at work or home & try to criticize a lot less. It'll make both of your lives easier.Honest and sincere appreciation is the most effective tool used sparingly by the majority of people. The effectiveness of this tool has been undermined by many due to various reasons. However, the people who have used it efficiently have done wonders in their personal and professional lives.

2

How to Become Friends With Someone (Fast)

"I'd love to make new friends, but I never know what to say or how to become closer friends with someone. I feel awkward during conversations and get really self-conscious. How can I learn to relax and bond with others?"

Friendships are great for our mental health, but it's not always easy to form a friendship bond with someone. In this guide, we'll look at some strategies to help you start and build a friendship. You'll also learn about a method that's been scientifically proven to build a bond between two strangers in under an hour and how to adapt it to real life when making new friends.

Show that you are friendly

If you want to make good friends, you have to be friendly and be approachable. A good friendship can do you so so much good. You can live a much better life just by having people you can call friends.

You can deal with day-to-day troubles easier if you have people to confide in. The company of friends makes celebrations much better celebrated. Even rising at the top of your career can become smoother if you have friends you can help with support, ideas, and even connections. You can never go wrong with having trustworthy friends.

Everyone makes friends in different ways, but aiming to be plainly friendly and approachable to others are the best ways to go about it. Everybody loves a friendly face and no one will hesitate going up to a person who looks approachable.

Just by having these two characteristics, you can drastically improve your social life. Not only will approaching other people become easier for you, but you can also be approached first.

If you feel like your "friendly" and "approachable" traits need to be improved, continue reading this article. Today, you are going to learn the tips and ways on how to be friendly, how to become more approachable, and finally, and how to use them to build friendships.

You need to know this before you continue. It doesn't take much effort to be friendly. But in this day and age, those who remain friendly despite the horrors of the world really are the strongest. Friendly people should be treasured and appreciated. Not everybody chooses to be friendly. You are a good person for actively trying to be one. You don't just make good friends by being friendly, you can influence those you meet to be better people.

1. Wear a smile. Always

A smile is the best thing a person can wear. Smiling frequently can help you appear more friendly, and it can cause you to be in a better mood. A lot of studies have done on this, and scientists have concluded that something as simple as smiling causes our bodies to release hormones that make us happier. So just by smiling, you can become a happier person. Once that happens, being friendly toward others will become more natural.

People will also have a more comfortable time being around you if they know you're a positive person. A smile is an indication that you're happy with where you're at and who you're with. Your positivity can even influence others. The people you're with will start to smile more if you do it first. You can influence the happiness of the group by doing something as simple as wearing a smile.

2. Greet people and start conversations

Don't be shy to approach people first. Great a person if you see one standing alone in a corner. Engage in a conversation with them. Get to know them personally. By taking your time to go up to a person and getting to know them, people will see you as the "friendly-type". It's one of the best reputations you can have.

If you're just walking down the street, or in a mall, or anywhere for that matter, whenever someone looks your way, greet them. Something as simple as a "good morning" or "hello" will be enough. So long as you take your time to greet that person, you are already actively being more friendly.

Do this as an exercise so when you actually go to a social gathering to socialize. You will have gotten so used to greeting people wherever you are that greeting people in parties will be like second nature to you.

3. Be mindful of your body language

Be mindful of how you stand. Don't slouch or cross your arms. Let your body project your feelings. If you slouch, you'll appear uncomfortable. Crossing your arms is a sign that your guard is up. If you want to appear friendly in public, just relax.

People will avoid making eye contact with you if your body language is off-course. They may think that you don't want to be there or are avoiding interaction with others, or they'll think you're just plain awkward. The goal of being friendly is to socialize more and socialize better. You won't have the chance to socialize if people avoid you or think you're trying to avoid them.

Let your arms free. If you feel uncomfortable with doing nothing with your hands, just place them in your pockets. Keep your head up and smile. When someone meets your eye, nod, and smile. If there's music, you can even move around to the beat. Let others know you're enjoying and that you're a positive person just through your body language. That's what you should aim for here.

4. Don't be afraid to break the touch barrier

This may seem very hard for you if you're uncomfortable with body contact, but breaking the touch barrier is something you need to do more if you want to be more friendly. Touch can say so many things words can't. Non-sexual touching is a sign that a person is comfortable with another person. You can simply tap the shoulder of another person, or grab their arm slightly, and they will feel easier being around you.

When someone tells a joke, you can grab their arm as you're laughing. If you're giving someone advice, you can place your hand on their shoulder. When telling your own story, if the story demands you to hold someone else, don't be ashamed to do it. Acknowledge the fact that touch can bring about emotions and there's nothing wrong with using it as a tool to connect with people. You'll appear more friendly and people will be more comfortable with you.

You also have to take note that this is something you should be mindful of. Break the touch barrier, but never go too far. That may go without saying but it's something that needs to be emphasized. Limit your interactions to friendly touches and you should be good.

5. Do your best to make everyone comfortable

Go out of your way to make sure everyone in your group is comfortable being there. If someone at a party is isolated and no one is approaching them, approach them yourself. If someone is who's part of a discussion is quiet, encourage them to speak up. You are acknowledging the fact that they mustered up the courage to attend that social event by building them up. They will feel grateful to you for helping them ease up a bit.

Make sure you find out as much as you can about them when approaching someone who's isolated at a party. Know their name, profession, interests, so on and so forth. This way, when you introduce them to a bigger circle, you'll know how to introduce them.

You can say something like "Hey everyone, this is Mike. He works in accounting. Don't ask him to do your taxes now". By doing something like this, you're making them feel included. You're letting the others know that he can be a part of this group and that you vouch for this person. You're the transition from isolation to being a part of a larger group. You'll appear very friendly AND people will appreciate you so much more.

6. Be empathetic towards others

You are an amazing company to have around if you can put yourself in the position of others. This is the essence of being empathetic. You can relate to the person you're talking to, you can talk to them the way they should be interacted with, thus having better conversations just by using your empathy.

Empathy is a friendly person's best tool. Being a proper friend is tough if you can't relate to other people, after all. You can really get to the bottom of what the other person is feeling and how they want to feel by paying attention to their body language and facial expressions.

You can figure out if they're happy or sad even before asking them questions about it. Start asking if it's necessary. Something as simple as "How are you doing, buddy?" goes a long way. If someone is feeling particularly gloomy, they will appreciate the fact that you took the time to ask them how they're feeling.

You can also figure out where to lead the conversation if you know how the person is feeling. If they're sad, you can direct the conversation towards happier grounds. If they're already happy to begin with, you can heighten that by making them happier. This is how you can be friendly by using your empathy.

7. Host your own parties

You can also appear more friendly by hosting your own parties instead of just attending parties hosted by others. This way, you'll be seen as someone who really likes by around other people. You're the kind of person who wants to be surrounded by friends and wants to make friends. You'll appear friendly.

People love being invited to parties. Even if they turn the invitation down, they'll appreciate the fact that you thought of them. In the essence of this, invite as many people as you can if you host your own party.

Invite your close friends and people you met at parties. Gather different circles of friends and make those two circles connect. Be a harborer of friendships. Make sure you offer food and drinks people will love. People will have a great time and they'll appreciate you for being a courteous host.

If you can't host your own parties, you can even simply ask other people out. Invite your friends to go out and have drinks, or have dinner, or watch movies. You can do anything so long as you're the one who's inviting, so take advantage of that. People will appreciate this just as much,

8. Be kind and respectful to everyone you meet

This is a very important rule of thumb, regardless if you're trying to be friendly or not. Be kind and respectful to everyone. It doesn't matter who they are or what they do, treat everyone the same way: with kindness and respect. If it's how you want to be treated, do unto others what you want others to do unto you.

You can also effectively improve your overall mood if you start acting kind and respectful towards everyone. You flush out anything negative you have in your system just by doing this. Therefore, you'll feel more inclined to be more friendly towards others.

If others see your acts of kindness, then good. It's good for your reputation as someone friendly. If not, then it doesn't matter. Keep being kind and respectful whether eyes are on your or not. Keep doing this until it becomes a force of habit.

9. Give compliments

Don't shy away from giving out compliments. Compliment other people on how they look, how they act, or for their thoughts. You can say something good about everything about a person. They'll feel good for being complimented, and you'll appear friendly for giving out the compliment.

You can use compliments as conversation starters too! For example, if you see someone wearing an incredibly beautiful suit or dress, you can go up to them and spark up a conversation, using a compliment as a starter.

Say something like "Hi there, my name is x. I love your suit! Where might I get myself one of those?".

You are actively starting the interaction and already lifting them up by doing something like this. The conversation can then proceed as usual, but they will always remember the fact that you started the conversation by complimenting them.

10. Be genuine

This is the most important part of being friendly — you need to be very genuine about it. Don't be fake when you're being friendly. A lot of people will be able to see through this, and you might even despise the act if you do it in the long run. However, you're genuine about being friendly, it will all flow naturally. If you actually want to be friendly, then you can be friendly. You'll make great friends and people will find you highly likable.

Just think about why you're doing what you're doing. Why are you doing your best to be friendly? Why read this article? What's the purpose of your research and why are you taking your time to study all of this? If you want to have a better social life, connect with people better, build friendships, and cause an overall greater impact in your life, then you're already on your way to being genuinely friendly.

If you hate socializing and you're trying to be friendly, it will never work. Maybe it will, but it will never be genuine. The first thing you should do is realize the importance of having great friends. You need to know that it can affect your life in a positive way. Then, you need to know that being friendly is one of the best ways to meet great people.

You want to be friendly because you want others to be happy when they're around you. You want them to be comfortable. You're trying to friendly not only for your own good, but for the benefit of others as well. Just think about all of this and being friendly will come fast, easy, and natural for you.

3

Criticism is futile

Do you know someone you would like to change in some way? When you find yourself getting caught up in other people's annoying habits or behaviors, think of a few reasons they might be acting the way they are.

Say to yourself, "I should forgive them for this because …" and conclude this sentence with an open mind. You'll be in a much better position to hold back from criticizing.

World famous psychologist B.F. Skinner proved that an animal rewarded for good behavior will learn much faster and retain what it learns far more effectively than an animal punished for bad behavior.

Since then, further studies have shown that this same principle applies to humans as well: Criticizing others doesn't yield anything positive.

We aren't able to make real changes by criticizing people, and we're instead often met with resentment. It's important to remember that when dealing with people, we're dealing not with creatures of logic, but with creatures of emotion, who are motivated by pride and ego.

1. GIVE PEOPLE WHAT THEY WANT

Why talk about what we want? That is childish - absurd. Of course, you are interested in what you want. You are eternally interested in it. But no one else is. The rest of us are just like you: we are interested in what we want.

Every single person is inherently self-interested. We tend to focus most on the things we want, and this fixation provides an incredible opportunity to influence people.

First, arouse in the other person an eager want. He who can do this has the whole world with him. He who cannot walks a lonely way.

This is perhaps the most pivotal lesson - the importance of seeing things from another person's point of view. For example:

Discovering what an employee really wants out of a job allows a leader to tailor that person's work so that it's highly engaging

Knowing exactly what someone is hoping to learn from an event allows a leader to craft the most relevant keynotes and seminars

Tomorrow you may want to persuade somebody to do something. Before you speak, pause and ask yourself: 'How can I make this person want to do it?'

2. SEEK FIRST TO UNDERSTAND, THEN TO BE UNDERSTOOD

Ninety-nine times out of a hundred, people don't criticize themselves for anything, no matter how wrong it may be.

Criticism is futile because it puts a person on the defensive and usually makes him strive to justify himself. Criticism is dangerous because it wounds a person's precious pride, hurts his sense of importance, and arouses resentment.

As leaders, it's easy to get frustrated when people mess up. From our perspective, it's often hard to see how or why a mistake has been made. The easy route in these circumstances is to find fault or nitpick.

That approach doesn't work, because people don't take well to criticism, no matter how justified it is. So, what's the better approach?

Instead of condemning people, let's try to understand them. Let's try to figure out why they do what they do. That's a lot more profitable and intriguing than criticism; and it breeds sympathy, tolerance and kindness.

This provides a far greater chance that the same mistake (or something similar) won't happen again.

Any fool can criticize, condemn and complain - and most fools do. But it takes character and self-control to be understanding and forgiving.

3. MASTER THE ART OF CONVERSATION

Isaac F. Marcosson, a journalist who interviewed hundreds of celebrities, declared that many people fail to make a favourable impression because they don't listen attentively.

'They have been so much concerned with what they are going to say next that they do not keep their ears open....very important people have told me that they prefer good listeners to good talkers, but the ability to listen seems rarer than almost any other good trait.'

Conversation is at the heart of every relationship. We all spend many hours talking to family, friends and colleagues. In the context of conversation, undivided attention is the highest compliment we can pay anyone.

Jack Woodford writes that:

Few human beings are proof against the implied flattery of rapt attention.

For many of us, good conversation implies being able to talk about lots of interesting facts and events. Nothing could be further from the truth.

If you aspire to be a good conversationalist, be an attentive listener. To be interesting, be interested. Ask questions that other persons will enjoy answering. Encourage them to talk about themselves and their accomplishments.

4

GIVE PEOPLE WHAT THEY WANT

Admit it. You're sick of being invisible with no clue how to grab attention. You'd prefer people hate you, because at least then people would notice, but the worst is when you're ignored.

How do you stand out in a noisy world with limitless choices? The answer is easy; provide value. The way to do it is shockingly simple: Give people what they want. Catapult your value game with these 52 phenomenal tips.

1. Admit your mistakes.

If you've ever been in a relationship with a person who can't admit they're wrong, you know the frustration. No one's perfect. Humility builds trust. Be quick to apologize and take responsibility.

2. Learn from others' mistakes.

I grew up in the ghetto and watched people throw their lives away through drug addiction and other vices. I didn't need to smoke crack to know it was a boneheaded move. Avoid other people's pitfalls, and shorten the learning curve. It's the quickest path to success.

3. Combine things.

Books and coffee, cookies and cream, sandwich meat and bread, flowers and chocolates, go well together. Amazing combinations can be obvious or unusual. When you combine great things, you create synergy and opportunities for exponential value growth.

4. Simplify.

As an author, I've learned efficient speech and straightforward plots are preferable to redundant words and confusing storylines. Stephen King agrees in his epic masterpiece On Writing.

The concept is the same in life. People want simplicity. Fancy features and limitless choices confuse and frustrate. Find ways to remove the clutter, and you'll save people time and effort.

5. Give business away to your competitors.

Refer people to others when it's a better fit. If you lack the expertise or ability to provide value, refer people to someone who can. It will engender goodwill from industry leaders and trust with future clients.

6. Surround yourself with successful people.

If you spend time with value experts, it will rub off. If you hang out with unmotivated losers, ditto.

7. Keep the focus on them.

Ever had a dinner date who wouldn't stop talking about themselves? How did you feel?

Too much focus on your desires cripples your awareness of those around you. Don't convince others of your greatness. Instead, learn what you can do for them.

8. Ask them.

Do you remember a day when everything went wrong? I'm talking epic bad day, one when you spilled coffee on yourself and hit all the lights on the way to work. You were certain nothing could change it. Then, something happened.

Someone noticed the frustration on your face. You didn't have to tell them. They simply asked: Is there anything I can do? With those few words, they disarmed you. They were sincere, and you knew it.

Learn to ask. You may not get the complete picture, but it's a starting point. From there, you can maneuver to find the right path.

9. Listen.

Ever poured your heart and soul to someone only to discover they weren't paying attention? You wanted their advice, but ended up frustrated and forced to repeat yourself.

Don't just hear what people have to say, actively listen. Better yet, write it down. Keep track of what people say most often. You will gain a clearer picture of what they want and how you can provide value.

10. Dig deeper.

As Simon Sinek would say, Start With The Why. Why do they do what they do? What's the desire that burns in their heart? We all have the same underlying emotions. We seek love, security, and acceptance. We have passion but are often stymied by fear. Behavior is a reaction to that emotion.

Discover the why, and you can service that need. Unveil the real reason behind people's actions, and you can fulfill their desires.

11. Ask other people.

People often lie to themselves and tell you what you want to hear. If you've ever been told how great you look in a dreadful outfit you get the idea.

Ask someone's friends to get a better picture. The principle is the same in business. Don't know how to fulfill a need? Ask someone with insight. People aren't always aware of what issue they want resolved, but experts can reveal what plagues the user.

12. Reflect.

Create a frequent sounding board for input. Reflection crystallizes the truth and minimizes self-deceit. Make reflection a regular part of business and relationships.

13. Accept gifts.

Ever see a kid's face light up after you gave them the perfect gift? Didn't it feel great? Don't be a Scrooge. Promote a sense of joy and connection. Accept gifts, and create opportunities for others to do the same.

14. Tell them.

Sometimes people need handholding. State how they'll benefit. Don't overdo it; just be honest and concise. That's effective marketing.

15. Be honest.

Honesty is hard, but so are most things that matter. Break through the fear barrier and tell the truth. You'll create trust and provide actionable advice. Your bravery will establish respect and a loyal following.

16. Research.

Discover if your idea is already being used and how many people you can help. What's required to launch your product, and what's the best pricing strategy? Research can direct you to other ideas you might have overlooked. A little research goes a long way.

17. Ask for help.

Don't be afraid to involve other people when your grand idea hits a snag in execution. Visionary brilliance is the foresight to share the load and forgo the desire to micromanage every minute detail of an operation.

Delegation is a priceless trait of successful people. Ask for help when you're stuck and allow humility to increase your value.

18. What's bothering you?

If you've ever experienced a frustration and wondered why someone didn't handle a problem that seemed simple enough to fix, you've stumbled on a potential way to add value. This is especially powerful when you have expertise in that specific field.

Don't let your frustrations go to waste. Use those obstacles as opportunities to give people what they want.

19. Eliminate problems.

Once you find problems, uncover ways to fix them. Don't sell yourself short and assume someone's already taken action. In relationships, it's all about problem-solving. The more you solve, the more you'll look like a guru.

20. Anticipate.

What new problems will products create? What issues lie down the road? Anticipate them, and you'll create more opportunities to provide value.

If you're great at anticipation, you can create solutions and services to your own pipeline of products. Printer ink is the perfect example. With no printer, there's little need for ink. Same goes for software and computers or apps and smartphones. Don't leave anything to chance; be one step ahead, and create the need.

21. What are other people doing?

What are successful people doing now to give people what they want? What about those in healthy relationships? Talk to people who've been together for decades and ask them their secret.

22. What's working now?

Discover what's hot, and you'll glimpse how to give people what they want. You can't chase every trend, but popular products reveal surprising insights and can steer you in the right direction.

23. Execute great service.

People want amazing service, so give it to them. Customer service has steadily declined, and that's a frequent event in new businesses. If you want to reveal ways to increase value, enhance your service. You can even charge more without losing loyal customers.

24. Learn from failure.

Failure is life's great teacher. Be smart and learn from those failures. Reflect on why they occurred and what you can do to improve in the future.

25. Smile.

Happiness is contagious. Always make an effort to smile.

26. Say thank you.

Be gracious. A simple thank you demands respect.

27. Write it down.

Record what works. Failure to keep track of what people like will transform your successes into tragic losses.

28. Repeat your successes.

It's a no-brainer, but you'd be surprised how many people don't bother to capitalize on past triumphs. Avoid the temptation of shiny objects in the distance. If someone liked something the first go-round, chances are they'll like it the second.

29. Say no.

You can't say yes to everything. Don't be afraid to say no when it's not an ideal fit. Select wisely so you can give people more of what they want.

30. Cut the cord.

Some relationships become counter-productive. Cut the cord and move on when you can't add value. It will save everyone valuable energy.

31. Mentor.

Take Jack Canfield's advice in The Success Principles, and supercharge your legacy. Help someone else avoid your mistakes and build on your successes. You'll both gain tremendous benefit.

32. Look for ways to improve.

Avoid complacency, especially in exceptional times. Take the opportunity to analyze your delivery, cost, quality, and features. What can you improve? What problems still exist?

In relationships, seek ways to be creative. Push yourself beyond your comfort zone. Leverage your successes or you'll get crushed when the wind shifts.

33. Think before you speak.

Before you hit send on that text or email, before you open your mouth to destroy someone who just insulted you, think about the impact of your words. Be the better person. Be specific about how they can improve, and do it without being destructive, or keep quiet until you can.

34. Think before you act.

Don't behave in a way you'll regret later. If you're upset, tired, or otherwise compromised, remove yourself from the situation. Return the next day with fresh eyes. You'll thank yourself later.

35. Test.

Don't let impatience keep you from testing the waters. Before you spend a boatload of resources, test out your idea in a small way. What doesn't work on a tiny scale has little chance on a larger one.

36. Be punctual.

Don't expect people to believe you value their time if you're late. You don't want your time wasted, so treat them with the same respect.

37. Slow down.

Added thought and reflection provides more value. Don't rush.

38. Pay attention to detail.

When you respect the little things, people will marvel at your extraordinary work.

39. Give your best effort.

When you do your best, you'll have the best opportunity to give people what they want. They'll also be more inclined to forgive you when you screw up.

40. Eliminate fears.

Research common objections. Eliminate the problems, and communicate the solutions. Fear elimination provides its own value, but it also disarms and creates opportunities.

41. Get personal.

Doesn't it feel fantastic when someone calls you by your name? Show a personal touch, and you'll be rewarded.

42. Drop an occasional note.

Create a regular system of thank-you and greeting cards to friends and clients. Mail them out on holidays, birthdays, and anniversaries. Sometimes it will be the only note they receive.

43. Don't over-promise.

Promise less. Follow Scotty's lead in the original Star Trek, who always told Captain Kirk it would take longer than it would to fix the problem. People will be pleasantly surprised when you over-deliver.

44. Keep your promises.

Once you promise, keep your word. Reliability is a must.

45. Be consistent.

Ever cut your hair at a salon with a different result each time? Did you keep returning? Customers want consistency. Don't expect to stay in business if you aren't predictable or reliable.

46. Use systems.

Michael Gerber's The E-Myth Revisited explains how systems prevent overwork, maintain quality and consistency, and allow for expansion. Effective use of systems creates maximum value. Ignore them at your peril.

47. Pay attention.

Has the blur of life distracted you? Ever broken free from that routine and woken up to dramatic change? Stay relevant and dialed into the needs of others. Pay attention to the subtle signs before they leave you behind.

48. Be flexible.

Adapt or become obsolete. Be like the blade of grass instead of the stiff branch. Give people what they want not what you want. Squash your ego. Be effective, and embrace the change.

49. Keep learning.

Flexibility requires learning. Everything requires learning. Transform your wasted time into opportunities for growth. Become a lifelong learner and you will help more people.

50. Set the example.

People are always watching, so model the action you want people to follow. Strive to behave like those you seek to emulate, and people will benefit from your example.

51. Don't give up.

You're guaranteed to fail if you don't try, so don't give up. When you persevere through the pain, you'll transform and grow. Eventually, you'll reveal the hidden path to added value.

52. Demonstrate integrity.

Trust creation is essential in any healthy relationship. Develop trust through principles of integrity: Honesty, fidelity, discipline, and excellence. Integrity will raise your game to the next level.

If you truly want to give people what they want, step up and take control. Don't go back to your same old ways. The ball is in your court. Make the change. Bury your fear, and take action.

5

Summary of How to Win Friends and Influence People

There are three fundamental techniques for handling people. They are kind of basic and unspecific, but MASSIVELY important whenever we're dealing with people. These simple techniques will be repeated throughout the book. In fact, many techniques will constantly be repeated in different principles. I'm pretty sure that Dale Carnegie did that on purpose to make things really clear and truly hammer these techniques into our mind through constant repetition. So, if you sometimes feel like you've already heard something before, that's how it should be. Let's start! Criticism is futile because it puts a person on the defensive and usually makes him strive to justify himself. Criticism is dangerous, because it wounds a person's precious pride, hurts his sense of importance, and arouses resentment. Criticism is dangerous. It puts a person on the defensive, makes him want to justify himself. Criticism also arouses resentment, and hurts that person's pride, feelings, ego, and sense of importance. If we criticize someone, that person will usually almost immediately start to resent us. "Who do you think you are?! Do you think you're better than me?! You couldn't have done it better either. Next time I will criticize you, too, you little know-it-all." This might be something they're thinking. Another thing that happens is that the person who gets criticized will start to justify himself. He will invent all kinds of reasons why it wasn't his fault, why he couldn't have done anything else, and that he tried everything he could. At best, that's the start of a hefty dispute, nothing else. That's leading us exactly nowhere. Even if someone KNOWS that he's probably wrong, he will still justify himself. What a HUGE waste of time and energy that could have been spared if a better way of handling such a situation had been used (we'll learn many better approaches in this book). Think about the last time you've been criticized for something. Didn't you immediately start to justify yourself? Be honest. You probably did, right? We all do it naturally. Another question. Did you like the person for criticizing you? Or did you resent the other person? Resentment, right? Again, this is our natural inclination. It's just how it works...

Let's realize that criticisms are like homing pigeons. They always return home. Let's realize that the person we are going to correct and condemn will probably justify himself or herself, and condemn us in return Ultimately criticisms will always come back to us in the form of resentment and condemnation. What we should do instead of criticizing is try to understand the other person. Be understanding and forgiving. Try to figure out why they do what they do. Try to see the situation from their perspective. This approach breeds sympathy, tolerance and kindness instead of resentment and justification. A great man shows his greatness by the way he treats little men. – Carlyle Criticizing, condemning and complaining is easy. To be understanding and forgiving takes self-control and character. (By the way, studies completely back up this point. They show that human beings learn much faster through positive reinforcement than through criticism or even punishment. Reward for good behavior works better than criticism for bad behavior.)

John Dewey, one of America's most profound philosophers, said that the deepest urge in human nature is "the desire to be important." What do we all want? We want to survive, to eat and drink, to sleep, to have enough money, to protect our children and loved-ones, to have sex... AND we want to feel important. Fairly often all of these basic wants are gratified – all EXCEPT a feeling of importance. One way to give people a feeling of importance, is by giving them sincere appreciation and encouragement. Letting them know that they are important, what they do is important, and that they are doing a great job (at whatever it is). Lincoln once began a letter saying: "Everybody likes a compliment." William James said: "The deepest principle in human nature is the craving to be appreciated." He didn't speak, mind you, of the "wish" or the "desire" or the "longing" to be appreciated. He said the "craving" to be appreciated. Everybody likes a compliment. Everybody likes a pat on the back. Everybody likes sincere appreciation. Everbody likes to know that what they do is important and that they do it well and that they should continue doing it. Remember from earlier that people respond much better to positive reinforcement (appreciation) than to criticism. Positive reinforcement gives us a feeling of importance and makes us want to do even better next time, while criticism kills our ambition. (Whenever I'm talking about positive reinforcements, compliments, and appreciation, I assume that these are meant sincerely.) The difference between appreciation and flattery? That is simple. One is sincere and the other insincere.

Dale Carnegie tells us we should never forget that all our associates are human beings and hungry for appreciation. When we can truly appreciate someone, we give that person a feeling of importance. We give him motivation, increase his self-esteem, and ultimately make him feel better about himself. When you think about it this way, it's really a no-brainer... it doesn't even cost a thing. So what are some easy ways to do this? We could compliment a co-worker on her great speech. Tell her that we really liked how confident she was. That we wish we'd also be as confident as her in front of a huge crowd. We could let her know that we got a lot out of it, that we learned a lot, that her PowerPoint slides were well put together, that she brought the point across very well... We can try to find little things that most people don't recognize but the person itself probably did on purpose. Maybe she's wearing shoes that match her trousers very well. We can appreciate someone's personality traits like patience, ambition, and honesty. We can compliment someone on his or her work ethic. We could tell that person that we realize how hard he or she is working. We can compliment someone's clothing style. Even a simple "Thank You" can do the job if it's expressed through sincere appreciation. Whatever it is... TRUE, FROM THE HEART appreciation is always welcome and satisfies a person's craving to be appreciated. It satisfies their need to feel important.

Why talk about what we want? That is childish. Absurd. Of course, you are interested in what you want. You are eternally interested in it. But no one else is. The rest of us are just like you: we are interested in what we want. So the only way on earth to influence other people is to talk about what they want and show them how to get it. This principle is absolutely KEY in influencing others. To convince someone to do something, we must tell them what they will get out of it. What's in it for them? How will they profit from this? How will this improve their life? They don't care about us, or why it's going to help us. They couldn't care less. What they care about is themselves and THEMSELVES ONLY. That's basic human nature. So to persuade someone, we must first be able to see things from their perspective. We must see things from their point of view. We must ultimately be able to convince them that it's in their best interest. In other words, we must arouse in the other person an eager want. Let's say we're trying to convince our kids to eat their broccoli. To convince the kids, we must think about reasons why they would want to eat it. Certainly not because it's healthy... they couldn't care less about that at their age. What we can do instead, is to paint a picture in their mind as to how their life will improve if they eat the broccoli. We can tell them that they will grow tall, strong, and handsome. That they will become great athletes because of all the nutrients in it. We can tell them that they will be the smartest kids in the class, and that the other kids will adore them for being so smart. The key is finding reasons why the other person would want to do it. Reasons why it would be in their best interest to do it. Let's pretend you wrote a book and want to sell it to me. If you just tell me, "Hey Nils, I wrote this awesome book. Do you want to buy it?" NOOOOOO! NO! NO! NO! I don't care and I don't want to buy it... Why should I? What's in it for me? How will this book help me? How will this book improve my life? How will it make me feel better? I don't know. I don't see how this book will add value to my life. So no thanks... Here's what you should tell me instead, "Hey Nils, I got this book that shows you how to make more money so that you can buy your dream house, dream car, and generally buy anything you want. It will also show you how to do X and Y so that you can achieve this and that and even more." NOW we're talking! NOW I'm interested. NOW I see why I might want to get this book. I see what's in it for me. I see how I will benefit from it... in other words, you aroused in me an eager want to buy this book from you. Tomorrow you may want to persuade somebody to do something. Before you speak, pause and ask yourself: "How can I make this person want to do it?" See the situation from the other person's perspective and find reasons why they would want to do it. How would they benefit from this? What's in it for them? How could I make them want to do it? In short: Arouse an eager want in them.

You can make more friends in two months by becoming interested in other people than you can in two years by trying to get other people interested in you. The premise of this chapter is pretty simple. We can make more friends by becoming genuinely interested in other people than by talking about ourselves and trying to constantly convince them how awesome we are. In a way we can learn this principle very well from dogs. What do they do when we get home? They couldn't be more excited and they greet as with sheer joy and enthusiasm. In other words, they show genuine interest in us. And it pays off for the dogs. They don't have to work a day in their life. All they have to do is give us love. The reason we like dogs so much, is the exact same reason why we like people. We LOVE people who are genuinely interested in us, who think we are good people, who seem to like us, and we especially love people who admire us. On the other hand, you may have some friends that are constantly talking about themselves, bragging about how awesome they are, trying to impress everyone, and never give you a moment of time to talk about yourself or your interests. If you are trying to speak, they aren't even listening properly. Instead they seem annoyed by the fact that you're now talking, and are waiting for any moment to take over the conversation again. Or even worse, they constantly interrupt you while you're talking. Ugh... I know some people who are just like that. I mean they are great people and all, but boy that is fcking annoying. I mean, give me a break! The problem with these people is that they show NO interest in us. That's why we don't like them as much as others. Okay, so what are some practical ways to show genuine interest in people? One thing we can do is to always greet others with animation and enthusiasm as if we would like to tell them something like "Hey, it's great seeing you again!" "I always enjoy seeing you." "I like you". "You're really cool and interesting!" "I appreciate knowing you!" We should greet people in a way that shows we're actually INTERESTED and EXCITED to see and talk to them. Another thing is to just genuinely be curious and interested in our conversations. If your opposite mentions the she's going to Spain in a few weeks, be curious and ask her about it. Where is she going? What is she going to do there? Why is she going there in the first place? Try to be interested in what she's talking about. If your buddy is talking to you about a book he just read and you feel that he really enjoyed it, ask him about it. What's the book about? Why did he enjoy it so much? Just let him talk about it and if the opportunity presents itself, ask a follow-up question. By doing that you indicate that you're truly interested in what he's talking about. Again, I emphasize that this interest should be GENUINE. Don't fake it...

Your smile is a messenger of your good will. Your smile brightens the lives of all who see it. To someone who has seen a dozen people frown, scowl or turn their faces away, your smile is like the sun breaking through the clouds. Especially when that someone is under pressure from his bosses, his customers, his teachers or parents or children, a smile can help him realize that all is not hopeless - that there is joy in the world. Actions speak louder than words, and a smile says, "I like you. You make me happy. I am glad to see you." I LOVE it! A smile brightens the lives of all who see it. A smile says

"I like you. You make me happy. I am glad to see you." Let's smile more often! Most of us are super concerned about how we dress ourselves, and about how we look in general. A quick look in the mirror before leaving the house is a must for most people. We want to look good for the rest of the world. What we often forget is that what we wear on our face speaks louder than what we wear on our bodies. Most people nowadays wear a frown on their face instead of a smile. People who smile tend to manage, teach, and sell more effectively, and to raise happier children. There's far more information in a smile than a frown. That's why encouragement is a much more effective teaching device than punishment. – James V. McConnell Smiles are powerful. They can completely turn around someone's day. I remember when I was in Brighton, UK, a few weeks ago. As I was walking down the street with my frown on my face (I was a bit nostalgic as I was thinking about old friends that I'd met there and not seen in a while), a man with a guitar walked towards me with a huge smile on his face. As he walked past me, he said, "Smile mate, the sun is out." That simple sentence and smile completely transformed my mood. Smiling is an easy way to make people like you. So whenever you go out, remind yourself of smiling at people. When you're buying something in a shop, smile at the cashier. When you're meeting your friends, smile and show them appreciation for being there. If you're at the bar ordering drinks, smile at the bartender. Even when you're on the telephone, smile because the person on the other end will notice it. Brighten the lives of others. Show them "I like you. You make me happy. I am glad to see you." What if you don't feel like smiling? You don't feel like smiling? Then what? Two things. First, force yourself to smile. If you are alone, force yourself to whistle or hum a tune or sing. Act as if you were already happy, and that will tend to make you happy. Action seems to follow feeling, but really action and feeling go together; and by regulating the action, which is under more direct control of the will, we can indirectly regulate the feeling, which is not. – William James Mood follows action. Keep that always in mind. If you don't feel like smiling, just force yourself to do it, and in no time you will be cheerful again and smile automatically.

Remember That A Person's Name Is To That Person The Sweetest And Most Important Sound In Any Language … the average person is more interested in his or her own name than in all the other names on earth put together. Remember that name and call it easily, and you have paid a subtle and very effective compliment. But forget it or misspell it - and you have placed yourself at a sharp disadvantage. Remembering and using someone's name is a great and incredibly simple way to make a person feel important. Dale Carnegie says that it's like making the other person a subtle compliment. Remembering and calling someone by his or her name is a bit like saying: "Hey, I remember you. I know you. You're important to me." Whereas forgetting someone's name is doing the exact opposite. It's like saying to that person, "Whoops! Sorry dude, who are you again? You're not that important to me." The WORST thing that can happen is to forget the name a couple of times and then have to ask the other person for the 4th time what his or her name is. At that point you've pretty much shown to the other person that he or she is not important to you. That person will probably think, "This is the fourth time that I see this guy and he still doesn't know my name? Wow, he must really give zero shits about me. What a douche!" Seriously. If you reconnect with someone you've met before and don't remember their name you're starting off on the wrong foot. Next time you meet someone, make a sincere effort to remember that person's name. If you don't fully understand, ask her to repeat it. If it's a weird name, ask her to spell it for you. If necessary, write the name down at the next possible opportunity. That's what Napoleon did. He would write the name down when he was alone, look at it, concentrate on it, fix it securely in his mind, and then tear up the paper. That's how important names are!

Good manners are made up of petty sacrifices. – Ralph Waldo Emerson Two things: 1. Remember people's names 2. Use their name when you're calling them or are in a conversation with them The second point is really important, too. If you meet someone for the first time, and use their name a couple of times during the conversation, you can be sure that this person will remember you. There simply aren't a lot of people who make the effort to do this. Anyway: Remember people's names and call them by their name. It's like telling the other person that he or she is important to you. In Dale Carnegie's words: It's like paying that person a subtle compliment.

Be A Good Listener – Encourage Others to Talk About Themselves If you aspire to be a good conversationalist, be an attentive listener. To be interesting, be interested. Ask questions that other persons will enjoy answering. Encourage them to talk about themselves and their accomplishments. Remember that the people you are talking to are a hundred times more interested in themselves and their wants and problems than they are in you and your problems. A person's toothache means more to that person than a famine in China which kills a million people. A boil on one's neck interests one more than forty earthquakes in Africa. Think of that the next time you start a conversation. People care mainly about themselves, their problems, their aspirations, their goals, and their interests. Oh and they LOVE talking about these things. All other things in this world are secondary. Especially other people's problems. Ugh... other people's problems. Who cares, right? Carnegie encourages us to let the other person do most of the talking. This way the other person can talk about all the things that he or she finds interesting, and doesn't have to listen to our problems which they usually don't care about anyway. What we can do while the other person is talking is to be genuinely interested, attentive, and possibly ask a few questions. Especially questions that we think the other person will enjoy answering. Again, it's not about us. It's about them. Carnegie tells a story from when he once attended a party where he met a botanist whom he found very fascinating. For hours and hours he was listening with excitement as the botanist was talking about his life and his passion (plants, gardens, flowers etc...), until the party ended and everyone went home. Before leaving, that botanist told the host of the party that Carnegie was an interesting conversationalist and he gave him several compliments.

Carnegie must have made a fine impression on the botanist. Funny enough, he hardly said a word for being called a good conversationalist. What he did instead was to show a genuine interest in the botanist and his passion. He listened attentively and let him do the majority of the talking. And so I had him thinking of me as a good conversationalist when, in reality, I had been merely a good listener and had encouraged him to talk. Again, that worked so well because people love talking about themselves and they love people who are interested in them. So, if they find in you someone who will genuinely listen to them and who is genuinely interested in what they have to say, they will LOVE you for it. (Btw, I'm NOT saying that you should waste hours and hours listening to someone you don't care about. These tactics work, but it's your job to figure when to use them and with which people.) Next time you have a conversation, try to pay attention to how much of the talking you do. Are you the one who's doing most of the talking or are you listening more? How are you listening? Are you actively listening or are you already thinking about what you're going to say next? Are you asking questions? Are you talking about yourself all the time? Or are you letting the other person talk about his or her interests, and problems? By the way, do you want to know a good way to make someone definitely NOT like you? If you want to know how to make people shun you and laugh at you behind your back even despise you, here is the recipe: Never listen to anyone for long. Talk incessantly about yourself. If you have an idea while the other person is talking, don't wait for him or her to finish: bust right in and interrupt in the middle of a sentence. Good stuff. Try it out sometime... You get the point: People care mainly about themselves. They LOVE talking about their problems, their struggles, and what's going on in their lives. If you want to make the other person like you let him or her do most of the talking and let them talk about themselves.

Talk In Terms Of The Other Person's Interests ...the royal road to a person's heart is to talk about the things he or she treasures most. Talking in terms of the other person's interests pays off for both parties. This one's straightforward. If we are in a conversation with someone it's generally a good idea to direct the topic to something the other person is interested in. That helps us find some common ground, connect, and build rapport with the other person. Let's pretend you know that Janine hates the military and is strongly against it. If you, on the other hand, are in favor of the military and think it's a necessity, what will happen if the two of you will start talking about the military? It will probably be a disaster and you'll very likely end up in a fiery discussion about who's right and who's wrong. One thing is clear: You won't become best buddies... If instead you know that you and Janine both love mountains, what do you think will happen if you start talking about mountains? The conversation will flow like crazy. You might say, "Mountains are awesome because they are so big and strong!" And she will respond, "Exactly! Mountains are so awesome. Did you ever hear about the Mount Prutu? That is the biggest mountain in Eastern Europe and ...." You guys will be in a lively discussion that both of you enjoy. And because you are both genuinely interested in the topic, it's very likely that you'll start to like each other. You've found common ground and are connecting and bonding. This is also especially important if you want something from someone. You can't just go up to that person and ask for it. It's much smarter if you first connect with that person or at least put that person in a good mood. That's exactly what will happen if you direct the conversation to something that they are interested in. Let them talk about it and you will notice that their mood is quickly improving. Then once they're in a good mood and like you for letting them talk about themselves and their interests, you can ask them. The odds are much better that they'll accept your offer, proposal, or whatever. Whenever Theodore Roosevelt (the 26th president of the United States) expected a visitor, he would stay up late the night before, find out what interests the other person has, and then read up on that. This made sure that he could direct the conversation to something that his visitor was interested in. Nifty strategy, eh? Here's another example you probably know from your childhood: Let's pretend you're a kid and for whatever reason you just broke your mother's favorite coffee mug. When are you going to tell her? Do you tell her when she's already stressed out, pissed off, or even angry because of something else? Or do you wait until she is in a good mood, generally happy and positive? As far as I can remember, I always waited until my mother was in a good mood, or until I had something positive to tell her beforehand (like a good grade at school). This is the same principle. What you could also do is ask the mother about something you know she loves to talk about. Ask her about that TV show she loves watching. Anything that boosts her mood will do. And only AFTER you've done that, you tell her about the broken mug. So, next time you're talking to someone, try to direct the conversation to something that the other person is interested in. You will soon see that the conversation becomes much more animated and enjoyable. (Especially for the other person, who will then, in return, love you for that.)

Make The Other Person Feel Important - And Do It Sincerely There is one all-important law of human conduct. If we obey that law, we shall almost never get into trouble. In fact, that law, if obeyed, will bring us countless friends and constant happiness. But the very instant we break the law, we shall get into endless trouble. The law is this: Always make the other person feel important. John Dewey, as we have already noted, said that the desire to be important is the deepest urge in human nature; and William James said: "The deepest principle in human nature is the craving to be appreciated." As I have already pointed out, it is this urge that differentiates us from the animals. It is this urge that has been responsible for civilization itself. You want the approval of those with whom you come in contact. You want recognition of your true worth. You want a feeling that you are important in your little world. You don't want to listen to cheap, insincere flattery, but you do crave sincere appreciation. All of us want that. This is important. We all crave appreciation and a feeling of importance. We all want approval. We all want to know that we're doing a good job, that we're good people, that other people like us, that they appreciate us, and that we're important. The question is: How do we make other people feel important? How can we nurture this deep desire in other people? (We've actually already discussed a few strategies in previous chapters.) One way to do it is to ask ourselves this question: What can I truly admire about this person? Let's say someone obviously goes to the gym often and has a lot of muscles. This would be a thing to admire about him. So in that case we could tell him, "Man, you're quite a machine eh?" "Those are some huge fcking arms!" "How often do you train in a week?" "I'm sure you're working hard for that eh?" This does so many great things on so many different levels. First, it gives him a feeling of importance. He gets appreciation and knows that all the hard hours that he spends in the gym get recognized by other people. This makes him already feel pretty good about himself. Second, by asking about his training frequency, you give him authority be implying that he must know a lot about working out. He can now teach you a bit about it. Third, he gets a chance to talk about something he's interested in. These are all great things for you. In that scenario it's almost impossible, that this person will NOT like you. That's how powerful this little strategy can be. Bottom line: Find something you can truly admire about another person and make him or her a sincere and honest compliment. This gives the other person a feeling of importance and makes him or her like you in turn.

In a Nutshell: Six Ways To Make People Like You ? Principle 1 - Become genuinely interested in other people. ? Principle 2 - Smile. ? Principle 3 - Remember that a person's name is to that person the sweetest and most important sound in any language. ? Principle 4 - Be a good listener. Encourage others to talk about themselves. ? Principle 5 - Talk in terms of the other person's interests. ? Principle 6 - Make the other person feel important- and do it sincerely.

How To Win People To Your Way Of Thinking Alright, so those were 6 ways to make other people like you. Now we'll change gears a bit and look at 12 principles to help you win people to your way of thinking. Let's go for it!

The Only Way To Get The Best Of An Argument Is To Avoid It You can't win an argument. You can't because if you lose it, you lose it; and if you win it, you lose it. Why? Well, suppose you triumph over the other man and shoot his argument full of holes and prove that he is non compos mentis. Then what? You will feel fine. But what about him? You have made him feel inferior. You have hurt his pride. He will resent your triumph. We MUST avoid arguments like the plague. There's nothing to win and everything to lose. How many friendships have been broken because of some silly argument? How many marriages have been divorced because of constant arguing? How much grief, sadness, resentment, hatred, hurt feelings, deaths, and even wars have been caused by some dumb arguments?

Carnegie makes the point that we can't win an argument. Even if we "officially" win, all we get is someone who resents us and probably waits for a chance to punch back. Think about it. The person who has lost the argument feels embarrassed, uncomfortable, hurt in his pride, and probably feels very angry towards you. The loser of any argument might think something like this: "So what!? You were right? Big deal! Did you really have to embarrass me in front of other people? Fcking smart ass! Just wait for payback! Revenge is sweet mother*****!" You made him feel inferior and as a result of that he now wants to punch you in the face... So, even if you are right, what will arguing about it yield? Why prove the other person wrong? Is that going to make the other person like you? Why not instead let him save face? Remember, you have nothing to gain (except a little ego boost maybe) by "winning" an argument and everything to lose.

Show Respect For The Other Person's Opinions. Never Say, "You're Wrong." You can tell people they are wrong by a look or an intonation or a gesture just as eloquently as you can in words - and if you tell them they are wrong, do you make them want to agree with you? Never! For you have struck a direct blow at their intelligence, judgment, pride and self-respect. That will make them want to strike back. But it will never make them want to change their minds. You may then hurl at them all the logic of a Plato or an Immanuel Kant, but you will not alter their opinions, for you have hurt their feelings. What happens when you tell someone that they're wrong? Instantaneously they will see it as a challenge and try to prove themselves right. They will start to explain and justify their side of things and the two of you will soon find yourselves in the middle of a heated discussion. (Which we try to avoid, right?) Usually such discussions are huge ego battles and everyone is trying to prove to the others and everyone else around that he's smarter, more intelligent, and most importantly: that he's RIGHT! What's worst about all of this: You have NOTHING to gain, except a little bit of ego gratification. If you DO prove them wrong "officially", then two things will happen. First, they will resent you, because you've hurt their pride and their feelings. (Similarly to when you "win" an argument) Second, they will do everything to still prove you wrong. They will want to strike back. They will not believe you, but they will try to find out that they were actually right. They might, depending on the disagreement, hit up google for a few hours to try and find that maybe they were in fact right. They will try everything to find out that they were right. Here's what will definitely NOT happen: They will NOT want to agree with you and they will NOT want to change their mind.

So what should we do instead? If a person makes a statement that you think is wrong - yes, even that you know is wrong - isn't it better to begin by saying: "Well, now, look, I thought otherwise, but I may be wrong. I frequently am. And if I am wrong, I want to be put right. Let's examine the facts." What a different reaction that will bring! Instead of using insulting phrases, we should start to use phrases that let the other person know that we understand them and respect their opinion. ? You're wrong! ? Terrible idea! ? That will never work in a million years! ? "Well, now, look, I thought otherwise, but I may be wrong. I frequently am. And if I am wrong, I want to be put right. Let's examine the facts." ? Well, that's possible. I thought that ... but you might be right. ? Hmm that can be, yes. I believe that ... but I might be wrong. We MUST try to see the situation from the other person's perspective. From the OTHER PERSON's perspective! If you tell him that his idea sucks, he may think to himself: "What an a**hole! I've spent 5 days coming up with that idea! I'm sure he doesn't have a better idea either! Let me prove to that guy what an idiot he is!" How is that ever going to help us? Hint: It's NOT! (Because we didn't respect his opinion.) When dealing with people, we have to be very careful not to hurt their feelings, pride, self-respect, or other sensitivities. We have to RESPECT their opinion and see the situation from their perspective. If you are going to prove anything, don't let anybody know it. Do it so subtly, so adroitly, that no one will feel you are doing it.

If You Are Wrong, Admit It Quickly And Emphatically There is a certain degree of satisfaction in having the courage to admit one's errors. It not only clears the air of guilt and defensiveness, but often helps solve the problem created by the error. Any fool can try to defend his or her mistakes - and most fools do - but it raises one above the herd and gives one a feeling of nobility and exultation to admit one's mistakes. Carnegie tells the story of taking his dog to the park without a leash, and then running into a police officer who scolded him, because it was against the law. Carnegie knew that his dog wouldn't like being on a leash so he let him run free again next time. He ran into the officer again and knew he would be in trouble. Instead of waiting for the police officer to scold him again, Carnegie spoke up first, apologized, admitted he was wrong, admitted that he shouldn't have done it, and that it won't happen again. The police officer was baffled and didn't really know what to say at first. Then he responded in a very soft tone, told Carnegie it was OK, that he was overreacting, and even told him to take his dog off the leash on the other side of the hill where he wouldn't see him. That policeman, being human, wanted a feeling of importance; so when I began to condemn myself, the only way he could nourish his self-esteem was to take the magnanimous attitude of showing mercy. I think that policeman also gained a feeling of importance by putting himself above the law by permitting Carnegie to let his dog off the leash on the other side of the hill where he wouldn't see him. Now ask yourself what would have happened if Carnegie didn't admit he was wrong and instead would have defended himself and tried to justify his decision. The two would have ended up in a bad discussion about whether that law makes sense or not and that everyone has to obey the law even if they don't think it makes sense blablabla... Would that have made the two best friends? Probably not. So, next time when you're wrong, admit it. Don't try to dance around it and attempt to sugar coat it. It's better to just admit your mistake, say you're sorry, and show contrition. Also, if you've made a mistake that might go unnoticed, challenge yourself to point it out and admit your mistake. That will save you a lot of energy than just waiting and secretly hoping that nobody will ever find out.

Begin In A Friendly Way If your temper is aroused and you go off on someone and tell them a thing or two, you might feel good afterwards, but how does that person feel? Do they want to agree with your points after you embarrassed them and attacked their pride? You're angry or frustrated at someone and your natural reaction is to go up to that person and tell them straight in the face what's going on. You unload your feelings towards them and properly tell them your opinion! Pheeew that felt great! You showed them what you're made of! That will teach them a lesson or two, right?!? Just think about the other person for a second. Is he going to like you? NOOOO! Not a little tiny bit! He will resent and despise you and wait for an opportunity for payback. We CAN'T force someone to agree with us. The sun can make you take off your coat more quickly than the wind; and kindliness, the friendly approach and appreciation can make people change their minds more readily than all the bluster and storming in the world. What we CAN do instead is to be friendly and kind like the sun. We can come in and say, "Hey, I think this didn't really work out as planned. Let's sit down, talk this through and see if we can make this right." In other words, we can begin in a friendly way. Let's pretend your landlord sends you a letter announcing that the rent will go up for the second time in a short period of time. You can't afford that! You're pissed and think that the landlord is a greedy pig. Your first idea is to go up to him and blast him for being so greedy. Then you stop and think and realize that this will never convince the landlord to lower the rent again. So you remind yourself of what Carnegie advises us to do instead: Begin in a friendly way. So here's what you do: You tell the landlord that you really like the apartment and neighborhood here. You tell him that he's really doing a good job running the place. You tell him all the good things that you enjoy. Maybe he's always quick to send over someone to repair something if it's broken or whatever. The point is: You start in a friendly way and only then you tell him that you would love to stay for another year or two, but simply can't afford it. Now, the chances are much better that he'll at least think about it. Very likely he'll now try to understand your position as well and then lets you get by with the lower rent. So, always start in a friendly way. Choose the friendly and kind approach. Be like the sun, not the wind. A drop of honey catches more flies than a gallon of gall. So with men, if you would win a man to your cause, first convince him that you are his sincere friend. Therein is a drop of honey that catches his heart; which, say what you will, is the great high road to his reason. – Abraham Lincoln

Get The Other Person Saying "Yes, Yes" Immediately

In talking with people, don't begin by discussing the things on which you differ. Begin by emphasizing - and keep on emphasizing - the things on which you agree. Keep emphasizing, if possible, that you are both striving for the same end and that your only difference is one of method and not of purpose. When we're talking to someone, we should always begin with the things we agree on. In fact, we should do that throughout the conversation. We want to constantly emphasize that we're in the same boat, trying to achieve the same goal, and that the only difference is one of method, not of purpose. We've talked about this quite a few times in previous principles. As long as you're talking about interests (or purposes) that you both share, everything is smooth and fine. Yet, once you start talking about things you disagree on, a fight is not too far away, and your chances of convincing that person of your way of thinking get smaller and smaller. The key here is to keep your opponent from saying "No", because that is a very difficult sentiment to overcome. Once the other person has said "No", his pride and ego are involved. He must now be consistent with his answer and his standpoint. Keep that in mind: A "No" is very difficult to overcome. Get the other person saying "Yes, yes" at the outset. Keep your opponent, if possible, from saying "No." A "No" response, according to Professor Overstreet, (*) is a most difficult handicap to overcome. That's why Carnegie suggests that we start by getting the other person to say "Yes, yes," as this moves the person in an affirmative direction. Let's say you're a kid and want to ask your mother if you're allowed to get a dog. What you wouldn't want to do in that situation is to just ask her straightforward, "Mom, can I get a dog?" This makes it way too easy for your mother to just say "No".And once she has said no, you're pretty much fcked. Instead, start by getting her to agree with you on a few things, similarly to this, "Hey mom! I just watched an awesome documentary about dogs. You know that I really love them, right (she should know and say yes)? And you know that I've always wanted to have a pet, right?" So, you get the point... you would make her say "Yes" to a few questions and then ask her if you could have a dog. That way, your chances should be much better. Whenever you want to ultimately get a "Yes" in the end, start off by getting a few "Yesses" first and getting the person to agree with you. Then that person is in affirmative, the conversation will be in an agreeable tone, and you're chances of getting your way are much better.

Let The Other Person Do A Great Deal Of The Talking Most people trying to win others to their way of thinking do too much talking themselves. Let the other people talk themselves out. They know more about their business and problems than you do. So ask them questions. Let them tell you a few things. If you disagree with them you may be tempted to interrupt. But don't. It is dangerous. They won't pay attention to you while they still have a lot of ideas of their own crying for expression. So listen patiently and with an open mind. Be sincere about it. Encourage them to express their ideas fully. That's not the first time that Carnegie advises us to let the other do most of the talking. It's because it's IMPORTANT... This is so true: When we try to convince someone of our ideas, plans, or whatever, then we usually talk, talk, and talk some more about why it's such a great idea and this and that and blablabla... Dale Carnegie says that this is the wrong approach, especially if the other person is angry, upset, or just sees things from a completely different perspective. By letting the other person talk, you show that you care and want to hear their opinion. If you interrupt them they won't listen anyway because they still have all their opinions and things to say running through their heads. Let them talk it out until they are "empty" and receptive for your perspective. So next time you're arguing with someone, let the other person talk herself out. Let her empty herself completely and see if that doesn't improve the situation DRAMATICALLY.

Carnegie makes another interesting point I want to share with you: Even our friends would much rather talk to us about their achievements than listen to us boast about ours. La Rochefoucauld, the French philosopher, said: "If you want enemies, excel your friends; but if you want friends, let your friends excel you." Why is that true? Because when our friends excel us, they feel important; but when we excel them, they - or at least some of them - will feel inferior and envious. This is important. Don't constantly tell your friends how awesome you are. Don't go like, "I'm so awesome. I just got an award for this and that. Man, I'm so great. Yesterday I worked incredibly hard. I made a 14 hour shift. How badass is that?! I'm so productive. I will be the king of the world!" You know what this will do? It will make your friends question themselves. They will realize that they HAVEN'T achieved as much as you. They will start to feel terrible about themselves and as a result of that, they will envy you and resent you. It's better to just follow Carnegie's advice and let your friends excel you. Let them feel good about themselves, instead of showing them their flaws and shortcomings. Let The Other Person Feel That The Idea Is His Or Hers Don't you have much more faith in ideas that you discover for yourself than in ideas that are handed to you on a silver platter? If so, isn't it bad judgment to try to ram your opinions down the throats of other people? Isn't it wiser to make suggestions - and let the other person think out the conclusion? Do you enjoy being told what to do? Fck no, right!? You prefer to think on your own. Independently. You have your own ideas. You don't need to be told what to do. Pfff... And guess what? Everybody else feels exactly THE SAME! We all prefer to have our own ideas and act on our own ideas. So why not use this to our advantage? Why not let the other person have the idea? Or at least let her think that it was his or her idea? If we care about the results, wouldn't that be the smartest thing to do anyway? Who cares if we get the credit or not? It's the results that count. If we have a great idea, we can try to make suggestions and lead the other person to that idea. If we're lucky the other person gets there, shouts "Eureka!" and is 100% convinced of the idea and 100% motivated to get that idea executed. GREAT! Now we're off to the races and the result is already almost achieved. Carnegie makes the example of Mr. Wesson who sold sketches for design businesses. After failing hundreds of times in getting one studio to buy his sketches, he changed his approach. He created a few incomplete sketches and asked the potential buyers what they would add to make the sketches useful for them. The stylists offered their ideas, Mr. Wesson completed the sketches accordingly, and in the end could sell all of them. If we truly care about the results, giving other people credit by letting them feel that it was their idea is a great way to accomplish the results we're after.

Try Honestly To See Things From The Other Person's Point Of View. Remember that other people may be totally wrong. But they don't think so. Don't condemn them. Any fool can do that. Try to understand them. Only wise, tolerant, exceptional people even try to do that. There is a reason why the other man thinks and acts as he does. Ferret out that reason - and you have the key to his actions, perhaps to his personality. Try honestly to put yourself in his place. This principle has made guest appearances in almost every other principle so far. As I said in the beginning many principles will start to overlap and become a bit repetitious. This is a good thing as it will really drive home the key principles we should be applying when interacting with people. This principle is at the absolute HIGHEST IMPORTANCE when dealing with people. We must understand that even if other people are completely wrong, they DON'T think they are. They think they're right. From their perspective they are acting logically. So we must always try to see a situation from their point of view. We must ask ourselves, "How would I feel if I were in his shoes? How would I react if I were in his shoes? What is he thinking? Why does he not want to do this? Why does he not like that? What does he believe about this? How will he react if I say XYZ? What will he think if I do this or that? What impact will this have on his life? How will this affect him? How will this change his situation? What would he like to get from this situation? What is his ultimate goal here? What is he trying to get out of this? If we do this and truly understand the other person's motives, interests, ways of thinking etc.... if we truly understand that person's point of view, then everything becomes much easier.

Of course this "understanding other people and seeing things from their point of view" won't happen overnight. It's a skill that must be trained like any other skill and I highly recommend you start developing that skill. It can save you a lot of time, energy, and frustration when dealing with other people.

Be Sympathetic With The Other Person's Ideas And Desires Three-fourths of the people you will ever meet are hungering and thirsting for sympathy. Give it to them, and they will love you. This is AMAZING!! People want to be listened to and most importantly: People want to be understood. People. Want. To. Be. Understood. They want to know that you understand their opinions and troubles. I remember when I was reading some diet book and found out that many overweight people are not at fault for their weight and that it's really fcking hard to lose weight. When I told this to my mom (for whatever reason she's always trying to lose weight, even though I think it's absolutely unnecessary as she isn't fat at all), her reaction was baffling, "I KNEW IT! DIDN'T I ALWAYS TELL YOU EXACTLY THAT?" She was completely happy. Almost ecstatic. Simply because I agreed on her point of view. Simply because she felt understood. Because I could now understand her struggles, understand that it's not her fault, and understand that it's fcking tough. Just as she's always been saying. (By the way I truly think that overweight people are usually not at fault for being overweight. However, just because it's not their fault, doesn't mean that it's not their responsibility to change it.) Carnegie also gives us a magical phrase that stops arguments, creates positive interactions, and makes other people listen to you attentively: "I don't blame you at all for feeling the way you do. If I were you, I would undoubtedly feel the same way." Here's what's great about this line: We can say it and be 100% sincere, because if we were the other person, in her situation, with her problems, needs, desires etc...,

then we would indeed feel the same way as she does. (Because we would actually be that person, right?) Here are a few similar phrases we might use... ? "Look, I totally get it. If I were you, I'm not sure if I would do it either..." ? "I don't blame you. I think it would be great if you could join us... But I understand it's a tough decision. I wouldn't know either in your situation." ? "Yep. I think you're totally right. If I were you, I'd probably feel the exact same way." The point is simple: People love feeling understood.

Appeal To The Nobler Motives A person usually has two reasons for doing a thing: one that sounds good and a real one. The person himself will think of the real reason. You don't need to emphasize that. But all of us, being idealists at heart, like to think of motives that sound good. So, in order to change people, appeal to the nobler motives. This is a pretty neat technique that you can use in many ways. The underlying premise is that we all have those two motives, the one that sounds good (the nobler motive) and the real one. Usually people themselves know quite well that they do something for the real reason, but why should we not make them feel great by emphasizing the nobler motives? If you know exactly that your buddy Mike does a certain job just for the money, but he tells you that he does it to help other people. Why on earth would you then tell him something like, "Aww come on, Mikey! We all know you just do it for the money. It's obvious. I mean it's OK, but you're a gold digger, bro!" Why would you emphasize the real motive? That's only going to make him feel bad and justify himself. Instead just let him have his nobler motive and be like, "Oh your new job? Yeah, I think it's pretty cool. I think you're helping a lot of people by doing that. It's definitely pretty cool." Appeal to the higher motive of helping people. That will make him feel good and put you in a good position to win him to your way of thinking. Or let's imagine your kids are having a dispute and you want them to stop. So you talk to the older brother and tell him, "Buddy, I want you to stop arguing with your little brother. I mean you're probably right, but he's your little brother. You are more mature. For me, you're like his bodyguard. His protector. You take care of him and are protecting him like great older brothers do it. He's looking up to you... you know that right? So stop arguing, and go play outside with him a bit." You're appealing to all kinds of higher motives: Maturity, protector, bodyguard, care-taker, being the ideal for his younger brother, being a great older brother etc... That kid will now try to fulfill

all of these personality traits that his father has "given" to him. He will stop arguing and go play with his younger brother outside (feeling like he's a great older brother). You can use this every time you want someone else to do something. ? Want your friend to start eating healthy ("You've always taken care very well of yourself....") ? Want someone to listen to you? ("You strike me as someone who's a great listener...") ? Want a friend to give you something? ("You're always so generous...") ? Want someone to do...? ("You know what I like about you? You're always so...") When you say such things, people will try to prove to you that it's true. "Oh yes, he's right! I AM a good listener." "Yeah, he's totally right. I have taken care of myself very well. It's only logical that I start working out." "Oh he's so right. I HAVE always been generous with other people. I can give him that..." Do you see how this works? The other person will always try to emulate the higher motive which you've assigned or given to him. Needless to say: ONLY use these powers for positive stuff and NOT to take over the world... I mean you've always struck me as a friendly, kind, and peaceful person anyway. So I probably wouldn't need to tell you, right?

Dramatize Your Ideas This is the day of dramatization. Merely stating a truth isn't enough. The truth has to be made vivid, interesting, dramatic. You have to use showmanship. The movies do it. Television does it. And you will have to do it if you want attention. We live in a world ruled by distractions. If we want someone's attention, we have to use showmanship. We have to DRAMATIZE (DRAMA Baby, DRAMA) our ideas in a way that wakes the other person up! It must be different, vivid, interesting, and dramatic. If a man proposes to a woman he goes down on one knee to show the importance of his feelings towards that woman. If you want to show that something is big, compare it to some other big thing. Show them a picture of the Eiffel Tower looking like a midget next to your new super tower. Instead of telling them how many acres big your field is, tell them how many football pitches that would equal. If your business is losing money on every sale, throw some coins on the floor to illustrate that. That will wake them up! The point is simple: If you want to get ATTENTION for your ideas or opinions, think of creative ways to make your message more INTERESTING, VIVID, , AND .

Throw Down A Challenge. Let Charles Schwab say it in his own words: "The way to get things done," says Schwab, "is to stimulate competition. I do not mean in a sordid, money-getting way, but in the desire to excel." The desire to excel! The challenge! Throwing down the gauntlet! An infallible way of appealing to people of spirit. That is what every successful person loves: the game. The chance for selfexpression. The chance to prove his or her worth, to excel, to win. That is what makes foot-races and hog-calling and pie-eating contests. The desire to excel. The desire for a feeling of importance. Have you ever heard of the expression Be the best - Fuck the rest? Most of us have this deep desire to achieve, to excel, to be better than others, to ultimately be the BEST. Nobody wants to lose. Nobody wants the consolation prize. Fck the consolation prize! We want to WIN! This principle is really straightforward. Carnegie says that if nothing else works, stroke that desire to excel and throw down a challenge. I remember when I tried to convince my younger brother to play with me (usually Super Smash Brothers on the Nintendo 64). The last thing I'd usually try was something like this: "Oh okay. You're just afraid to lose, because you know you have no chance. It's OK. I'm just too good for you. No, seriously. It's OK. Nobody likes to lose all the time." Funny enough, this shit worked incredibly well (especially when he was still younger. Today? Not so much anymore). Anyway, next time you want someone to do something, throw down a challenge and appeal to their need to excel. Tell your kids whoever eats that broccoli the fastest gets more dessert. Tell your salespeople whoever makes the most sales gets a bonus.

Tell your twin babies whoever shits in their pampers less often, ge... (lol, never mind!) You get the point: Nobody likes to lose, but everybody LOVES to win and be the BEST. If you want someone to do something, it can help to appeal to his or her need to excel and throw down a challenge.

Begin With Praise And Honest Appreciation Beginning with praise is like the dentist who begins his work with Novocain. The patient still gets a drilling, but the Novocain is pain-killing. It is always easier to listen to unpleasant things after we have heard some praise of our good points. Let me repeat that: It's always easier to listen to unpleasant things after we have heard some of our good points. So, when we're trying to correct someone's mistake or criticize that person, then we should always start by talking about the good things, the things that the person did well. You can almost view it as a sandwich. The bottom layer is the praise, the middle is your criticism, and the top layer is something positive (like praise) again. It's crucial that the praise is meant SINCERELY. You can't just say, "Overall it's good, BUT this and that and this here and there... these things all suck! You have to fix these things! Oh, but overall it was good..." That won't do the trick. You must do it in a sincere way and in a way that the other person understands it. Point out the details and little things that you liked, "This first part was great. You clearly did that very well and you added XYZ. It's well stated and you even did this other thing too which I thought was great. In part 2 there are a few things that I would like to have a closer look at (then start with constructive criticism)." Remember that we all CRAVE appreciation. If we've done something right, please let us know and show some appreciation for it... If you're in a leading position (mother, father, boss, team leader, coach, etc...) and have to criticize someone, always start with praise and the things this person did well. After that it's much easier for the other person to listen to unpleasant things.Call Attention To People's Mistakes Indirectly Charles Schwab was passing through one of his steel mills one day at noon when he came across some of his employees smoking. Immediately above their heads was a sign that said "No Smoking." Did Schwab point to the sign and say, "Can't you read?" Oh, no not Schwab. He walked over to the men, handed each one a cigar, and said, "I'll appreciate it, boys, if you will smoke these on the outside." They knew that he knew that they had broken a rule - and they admired him because he said nothing about it and gave them a little present and made them feel important. Couldn't keep from loving a man like that, could you? Calling attention to one's mistakes indirectly works wonders with sensitive people who may resent bitterly any direct criticism. We already know that when we want to correct someone, we should start with praise. That's great. Unfortunately, most people follow that good start with the dreaded B word... you know the word... "BUT". Ugh. Ugly, ugly word. Personally, I try to use it as little as possible. I know they say we shouldn't judge words, but boy does this little sucker do a lot of harm, or what?! It all starts off so well, "Patrick we're really proud of you. You've gotten much better grades this year. But if you worked a bit harder, you could do much better." Patrick might be encouraged and feel pretty good about himself, UNTIL he hears the word "but". This immediately makes him question the sincerity of the initial praise and he will wonder if that praise wasn't just a contrived lead-in for the parent's criticism. The word "but" can in certain situations completely nullify what has been stated before. Remember this example: "Overall it's pretty good, BUT... (uh oh... here comes the real feedback)" That "overall it's pretty good" gets completely nullified by the following "but". Carnegie advises us to change this ugly word to the much more beautiful word "and". Let's see what that'll do: "Patrick we're really proud of you. You've gotten much better grades this year, and if you work a little bit harder next semester, you will do even better." Now we're talking! In this situation there is no direct criticism. Instead there is POSITIVE REINFORCEMENT and the acknowledgment that he can do even better next time. Remember that positive rewards work much better for changing people's behavior than negative criticism. Next time you have to correct someone, don't use the word "but" and use the word "and" instead. Give criticism in an indirect, positive, and uplifting way.Talk About Your Own Mistakes Before Criticizing The Other Person It isn't nearly so difficult to listen to a recital of your faults if the person criticizing begins by humbly admitting that he, too, is far from impeccable. Admitting one's own mistakes - even when one hasn't corrected them - can help convince somebody to change his behavior. This is another technique to kind of soften our criticism. We let the other person know that we understand them, that this happened to us as well when we were younger, or that it would have happened if we had been in a similar situation. This shows the other person that he or she isn't a complete idiot. Also this gives you a good chance to improve your relationship with that person. You can tell her a funny story from back when you made the same mistake; or maybe your mistake was even worse. So you totally get it that this mistake can happen, and you tell her that next time she should just remember it and do it better. You can use phrases like: ? "I would have done the same thing in your position." ? "You couldn't have known better." ? "I didn't know that either when I first started out." ? "It's totally normal to make such mistakes" ? "No worries, such things can happen. Happened to me many times when I was at your age (or in your position, or whatever)" Whatever it is... just let the other person know that you make a lot of mistakes too and show him that he isn't completely retarded for making that mistakes. Let him know that it's OK. That it would have been smarter if he had done it the other way, and that it's good that he now knows and can do it better next time. If you can use a personal story - even BETTER! This will help the two of you bond and strengthen the relationship.

Ask Questions Instead Of Giving Direct Orders Asking questions not only makes an order more palatable; it often stimulates the creativity of the persons whom you ask. People are more likely to accept an order if they have had a part in the decision that caused the order to be issued. No one likes to take orders. Nobody likes being commanded around and hearing "Do this", "Don't do that" all the time. You're not a dog, right? So what Carnegie tells us to do instead of commanding, is to ask questions or find another way to kind of bring them to the conclusion that it's the best action to take from their perspective. By asking questions we give people the chance for coming up with the conclusion themselves. We kind of give people the opportunity to do things themselves. If they think they've had a part in the decision, then they are much more motivated and likely to do what you would like them to do anyway. Here are a few examples you may want to copy: ? "You might consider..." ? "Do you think that would work?" ? "Do you think that would be a good idea?" ? "Do you think it would be smart if...?" ? "Do you think it would be smart to...?" ? "Maybe if we were to do it this way it would be better. What do you think?" ? "Maybe we could add..." ? "One could probably also do..." ? "You may want to..." These suggestions are much nicer than "Do this or do that!" or "Don't do this or don't do that!"

Next time you want to give orders to your wife, kids, employees, or co-workers try to ask questions instead of giving direct orders.

Let The Other Person Save Face Letting one save face! How important, how vitally important that is! And how few of us ever stop to think of it! We ride roughshod over the feelings of others, getting our own way, finding fault, issuing threats, criticizing a child or an employee in front of others, without even considering the hurt to the other person's pride. Whereas a few minutes' thought, a considerate word or two, a genuine understanding of the other person's attitude, would go so far toward alleviating the sting! This is a principle that really is near and dear to my heart. If we have a choice of either exposing someone or letting him save face, then why would we EVER choose to expose that person? Why would we CHOOSE to make him feel bad about himself? Why would we embarrass him? Why would we hurt his precious pride? What have we got to gain??? It's CRAZY! If we have to deliver bad news, negative feedback, or whatever it is, then we ALWAYS have a choice about how, where and when to do it. And we can ALWAYS choose to let the other person save face by not doing it in a way that will hurt his feelings, ego, or pride. For example, if we have to criticize someone, then we don't have to this in front of other people and completely embarrass that person. This person will feel TERRIBLE and condemn us in return. PLUS he or she is now waiting for a chance to pay us back. (We've talked about this in previous chapters.) Another example: If we know we're right about something and the other person is wrong. We don't have to rub it in the person's face in front of other people and make him feel inferior and embarrassed about it. We can keep it for us. Let him save face. Be the bigger person. Even if we are right and the other person is definitely wrong, we only destroy ego by causing someone to lose face. The legendary French aviation pioneer and author Antoine de Saint-Exupйry wrote: "I have no right to say or do anything that

diminishes a man in his own eyes. What matters is not what I think of him, but what he thinks of himself. Hurting a man in his dignity is a crime." Hurting a man in his dignity is a crime. There is absolutely no reason why we would have to make other people feel bad about themselves. By the way, you can use this principle in a lot of situations... Let's say you're in a group of people and someone made a huge mistake and the others are making fun of him. Here you could give your opinion in a way like this: "What are you guys talking about? This could happen to any of us. After all, it's not such a big deal either. I mean who cares if..." This approach takes the heat out of the situation and the center of attention off the person who made the mistake. You better believe that this person will be HAPPY and GRATEFUL you did it. My point is: If we have the CHOICE to make a person feel good or bad about themselves, we should always choose to make them feel good. Most people have low self-esteem already, so there's absolutely no need to crush them down even further.

Praise The Slightest Improvement And Praise Every Improvement. Be "Hearty In Your Approbation And Lavish In Your Praise." Remember, we all crave appreciation and recognition, and will do almost anything to get it. But nobody wants insincerity. Nobody wants flattery. Use of praise instead of criticism is the basic concept of B.F. Skinner's teachings. This great contemporary psychologist has shown by experiments with animals and with humans that when criticism is minimized and praise emphasized, the good things people do will be reinforced and the poorer things will atrophy for lack of attention. Again, this is all about how you make other people feel. By using praise as your instrument you make them feel appreciated, important, and good about themselves. Praise is like sunlight to the warm human spirit; we cannot flower and grow without it. And yet, while most of us are only too ready to apply to others the cold wind of criticism, we are somehow reluctant to give our fellow the warm sunshine of praise. – Jess Lair We've talked about this before: Positive rewarding works much better to change a behavior than negative criticism. Carnegie says that the good things people do will be reinforced by praise and the bad behaviors will atrophy for lack of attention. Carnegie also makes the point that when we're praising someone we should do it SINCERELY and do it AS SPECIFICALL AS POSSIBLE. If we find specific things to praise, then it will automatically sound much more sincere. Instead of saying "Good job, very good presentation," say something like this, "Great presentation. I really liked your confidence and charisma up front. You stood there in a way that... Also, you made your points very clear. You made sure that they were always emphasized by doing XYZ and you also did XYZ which was very good." See how sincere that sounds? And how useful it is? That's how we should praise people: SINCERELY AND SPECIFICALLY. Oh, and here's another thing: We should praise often. Whenever we find the smallest improvement, we should highlight it. This way the other person realizes that we also notice the tiniest improvements and details. This reinforces their behavior. It lets them know that they're doing it right and that it's appreciated and noticed.

Give The Other Person A Fine Reputation To Live Up To In short, if you want to improve a person in a certain aspect, act as though that particular trait were already one of his or her outstanding characteristics. Give them a fine reputation to live up to, and they will make prodigious efforts rather than see you disillusioned. Do you remember this principle: Appeal to the nobler motives? And this example: "You strike me as someone who's a great listener..." (If you want that person to listen to you)? It's the same here: If you give a person a lofty reputation to live up to, this incites in them a desire to meet those expectations. In other words, act as though that particular trait were already one of his or her outstanding characteristics, and this person will try to live up to that. So, in the previous example that trait would simply be "good listener". This friend will now try to live up to that reputation and listen to you. Assume a virtue, if you have it not. – Shakespeare Carnegie makes the example of a guy named Bill, a mechanic whose work had become unsatisfactory. Here's what his boss said to him in the situation: "You are a fine mechanic, you have been in the business for many years, and we've had a number of compliments on the good work you have done. But lately, your work has not been up to your own old standards, and I thought you'd want to know since you've been such an outstanding mechanic in the past." Want to know what happened then? Bill the mechanic found back to his old work ethic and became as good in his job as ever before. No wonder when you consider the reputation his manager gave him to live up to This doesn't just work when someone isn't doing as well as they can. In fact, it works in almost every situation. If you want to change someone's behavior, act as if that person already acted that way. You can use phrases like this: (Just fill in the blanks with whatever personality trait, habit, or action you want them to convince of.) ? "I really love _______ about you." ? "You're so good at _______. I think that's just great!" ? "You know what I appreciate about you? You always _________." ? "Why are you acting this way? Usually you're totally _______." Isn't this MANIPULATIVE? Yes, I guess it is. But aren't we always trying to manipulate each other? Let's say you're dead sick and don't want to go to the doctor. Wouldn't it be in your interest if the other person tried to persuade manipulate you into going to the doctor? After all, if the other person can't convince manipulate you, your health might suffer dramatically. Or say you would like to go for a jog with your best friend. When you're trying to convince him of doing that, you're manipulating him as well. We're really manipulating each other all the time, so we might as well learn some tricks to do it better and more efficiently. After all, we're the ones who aren't using it for evil anyway .

Use Encouragement – Make The Fault Seem Easy To Correct Tell your child, your spouse, or your employee that he or she is stupid or dumb at a certain thing, has no gift for it, and is doing it all wrong, and you have destroyed almost every incentive to try to improve. But use the opposite technique - be liberal with your encouragement, make the thing seem easy to do, let the other person know that you have faith in his ability to do it, that he has an undeveloped flair for it - and he will practice until the dawn comes in the window in order to excel. This one's BIG. Let's say you're a dance teacher and you get a new client who just CAN'T dance at all. He's terrible at it. So, how do you talk to him? I'll give you two options: OPTION A: "You're doing it all wrong darling. Forget everything you've ever learnt about dancing. We'll have to start completely from scratch with you." OPTION B: "Well, your dancing style is a bit rusty, but the fundamentals are all right. We will surely make a pretty decent dancer out of you. I mean, that move from earlier was already really good." Approach B will work much better. Why? Because there you focus on encouraging. Maybe he's not a great dancer yet, but who is born that way, right? You assure him that he will learn it and praise the little things that he's already doing right. In other words, you use ENCOURAGEMENT. Approach A does the exact opposite. It says that he has absolutely no talent, does everything wrong, and tells him that he probably won't ever become even a halfdecent dancer. This approach is discouraging and focuses on all the guy's mistakes. I mean come on... We'll have to start completely from scratch with you. Just with you. The others are better when they start. They have talent. You don't...

Remember: Positive rewarding (praise and letting him know that he'll do fine) works better than negative criticism (doing it all wrong, completely start from scratch with you, no talent). So let's try to encourage our friends, family members, children, etc... Let's focus on what they're doing right and let them know that we believe in them. That's what will motivate, inspire, and get them into action.

Make The Other Person Happy About Doing The Thing You Suggest. One of the important rules of human relations: Always make the other person happy about doing the thing you suggest. Always make the other person happy about doing the thing you suggest. Very straightforward... If you give a task to an employee, tell him or her that it's a very important task to you and it's crucial the task will be well done. By doing that you tell your employee that he has responsibility and what he does is important. He will then be happy about doing that task. You can tell your kids that you will play something with them if they finish homework. Because they want to play with you, they will first happily do the homework. If you want anyone to do anything, try to give them an incentive so that they are happy about doing it. If, for example, you want your daughter to clean her room, find a way so that she'll be happy to do it. Tell her that when the room is clean there's much more space to play, she'll find all of her toys again, and will generally be in a better mood because... (who knows? I'm not a father...) I think you can use a lot of the previous principles to come up with ways to make the other person happy about doing the thing you suggest. You'll just have to be a bit creative. Bottom line: When you try to make another person do something, find ways so that he or she will enjoy doing it..